a Circus *without* Elephants

If you enjoy this book...

Please write a review on Amazon.com

Reviews work miracles.

I love giving speeches!

Contact me: Maralys@Cox.net

a Circus *without* Elephants

MARALYS WILLS

www.ivyhousebooks.com

Advance Praise for *A Circus Without Elephants*

"A beautifully-written family saga. Maralys Wills' deeply moving story of her family's triumphs and tragedies is a page-turner that I couldn't put down. I laughed out loud, wept tears of sadness and empathy, and became so engrossed with each and every member of the family that I felt bereft when I came to the end of their story. As compelling as any novel, *A Circus Without Elephants* paints word pictures of a wonderfully unique family. . . Evocative, funny, heart-breaking, the Wills family story is unforgettable."

—JOAN DIAL
Author of *Roses in Winter*

"Maralys Wills' memoir, *A Circus Without Elephants,* is a wonderfully funny book. Maralys has a wry, kooky sense of humor that turns life into one big, zany adventure, and then she takes ordinary life and shows us its ridiculousness and incongruities. Yet she never lets us forget the warm family love that surrounds her in this very funny odyssey—with feisty, independent children and a patient, sometimes perplexed husband. In a time of atom bombs, world assassins, ecological disasters, and racial hatred, Maralys shows us the sanity of everyday love, and that somehow we will endure through it all. So read her book, forget the world, and laugh."

—DR. PATRICIA L. KUBIS
Emeritus Profesor of English, Orange Coast College

"Maralys Wills is a writer with the perfect family. They constantly provide her with material which she utilizes to the fullest to keep her readers roaring with laughter, sympathizing in her predicaments and joining in her tears. *A Circus Without Elephants* is a must read for everyone who's ever been a parent or ever plans on that joyful eventuality. Bear in mind that a sense of humor is a necessity for the job."

—JAN MURRA
Author of *Cast Off*

PUBLISHED BY IVY HOUSE PUBLISHING GROUP
5122 Bur Oak Circle, Raleigh, NC 27612
United States of America
919-782-0281
www.ivyhousebooks.com

ISBN: 1-57197-449-0
Library of Congress Control Number: 2005901530

Printed in the United States of America

To Bobby and Eric,
who fell out of the sky too soon,
and to the survivors
who carry on with their joie de vivre.

Other Books by Maralys Wills

Manbirds: Hang Gliders and Hang Gliding
Tempest and Tenderness
Mountain Spell
A Match for Always
Soar and Surrender
Fun Games for Great Parties
Higher Than Eagles
Scatterpath
Save My Son

ACKNOWLEDGMENTS

To my agent, Pat Teal, a warm thanks for cheerful assistance all the way.

To the many readers who offered serious critiques, great ideas, and welcome enthusiasm, I am deeply indebted. I needed all of you. The following people were invaluable: Jan Murra, who spotted some important gaps and made a monumental difference, pointing me in the right direction. John Walsh, who gave me an honest appraisal that prompted some rethinking. Jobe Lawson, who gave the project some serious time. Erv Tibbs, whose keen ear for the rhythms of writing, consistent friendship, and willingness to re-read have buoyed me up on a hundred occasions.

To my early critique group: Pat Kubis, June O'Connell, Dorsey Adams, and Win Smith, warmest thanks for helping launch the first go-around. To my current critique group: Michelle Lack, Barbara French, Walt Golden, Pam Tallman, Allene Symons, and Erv Tibbs . . . What would I do without you?

To Christy Wills Pierce, Betty-Jo Wills, and Ken Wills, deepest thanks for your patient re-reads and many important suggestions.

To readers Pat Walker, Joan Dial, and Susan Hawkins, your enthusiasm made the whole effort seem worthwhile.

To Anna Howland and Tami Stoy of Ivy House Publishing Group, thanks for making the publishing process so enjoyable.

And last, to my husband, Rob, my heartfelt gratitude for story critiques that were endless and profound. Only you could have caught so many critical "fixes"—or come up with such an inspired suggestion for the title.

A Word to the Reader

SOMEHOW I'D GOTTEN myself in quite a mess.

As the mother of enough rowdy children to rival the nursery rhyme mother and her shoe, I should have been used to messes. But those days had slipped away and messes had become infrequent and I wasn't really expecting them now.

Yet here I was, late at night, with my legs straddling a wrought-iron fence and a deep-throated male voice from a house alarm bellowing threats so intimidating they made me weak. I was filled with a despairing sense that any minute the cops would come, lights blazing, and find me impaled on my son's fence. They would assume, of course, that I'd robbed the house and was trying to escape over the wall—and they'd shoot me dead.

Oh, it was a bad scene, all right.

I can't even say it's the worst ball-up I've ever been part of. It was just more memorable than most.

With bad luck and a few odd circumstances, I'd put myself in this predicament for the most innocent of reasons: I was trying to retrieve a twenty-eight pound Thanksgiving turkey—a beast so outlandishly big I hadn't especially wanted it in the first place. The bird had been nesting comfortably in my son's garage refrigerator, and God knows that's where it should have remained.

But, typical of my life, the simple act of trying to reclaim what was mine had turned so crazy that I became the central character in an ever-worsening drama: from my son's house alarm blaring threats, to the turkey turning slippery and becoming impossible to carry, to a gate that decided to stick and refused to let me drive away . . . and on to this scary midnight climb over a wrought-iron fence, and finally, of course, to the arrival of police. At the time it all seemed unimaginable, so bewildering, in fact, I was ready to abandon that miserable bloat of a beast and dine with my family at Jack-in-the-Box.

For a while I couldn't even smile about it. But at least I didn't get shot.

Days later my writer self surfaced. When I finally wrote the story I dubbed it "The Turkey Burglar," and my friends and family thought the incident was funny as hell and kept telling me how they laughed hysterically.

Oh well, I thought. *Anything to amuse my little cadre of readers. Anything to wring a laugh out of disaster.*

MY HUSBAND, ROB, and I are the parents of five boys and a girl. When our oldest was eight, we were lucky enough to find one of those scarce half-acre lots in southern California, and luckier still that it backed up to an orange grove. The kids grew up thinking there was nothing more exhilarating than waging war in a citrus grove and pelting each other with oranges. With so many boys and one tomboy girl under the roof, the masculine energy in our house became palpable; the floors vibrated with pounding feet and the walls shivered with noise. There was never any peace. But neither was there boredom.

As a couple of bookish students, Rob and I never imagined we would create a family of athletes, yet somehow we did. Our six kids played so many sports that one weekend they competed in five different counties. Two of our sons became pioneers in the fledgling sport of hang gliding—so exotic back in the seventies that the two were featured in *Sports Illustrated.* Our daughter played tennis at Wimbledon. And on Christmas Eve our fourth son, a butterflyer on a high-powered swim team that sometimes hosted foreign Olympians, brought home three carloads of Russian swimmers and their coaches—and two mysterious men who were obviously the KGB.

ALL THOSE YEARS I was scribbling little vignettes. This book is a compilation of the best of them.

But one important feature of our lives has been minimized. As anyone who knows us would probably mention, we've had our share of tragedies. Back in those early days of hang gliding, we set a record for family disasters that nobody would want to emulate.

I relived those awful days in detail in an earlier book, *Higher Than Eagles*, a memoir that covered both the exhilaration and the tragedy of a sport so seductive that it swept us away. Everything sad has already been said; I wrote and I cried and I poured out my feelings. It is done, and the worst parts of those grim days do not need to be re-visited—at least not in their entirety.

This is a different sort of book. Lighter, broader, and brimming over with incidents that never felt right for the earlier book . . . just as the full extent of the tragedies do not feel right for this one.

Readers will surely forgive me for sticking with a tone that suggests our lives have been mostly amusing. Well, mostly that's true. Because, along with sadness, happiness is surely our other reality.

Chapter One

The Maverick "Hawaiian"

I DIDN'T GO to Stanford University to find a husband.

I went partly because of the wondrous Stanford mystique and the thrill of calling myself a Stanford Indian . . . and partly because it was such an exclusive, snooty-tooty institution, if you got accepted you certainly had to go.

Before long, though, I was swept away by classes like Western Civ, where we dug around in the archives to unearth surprisingly modern truths from Plato and Aristotle, and by Russian History as taught by a guttural Russian. The campus beguiled me with its genteel Spanish Mission architecture, and I was soon rooting passionately for the plucky and gentlemanly, if somewhat inadequate, football team.

But I didn't stay long, only a year and a half, not nearly long enough.

And what I got out of it, eventually and to my surprise, went far beyond what I expected.

IN MY TREMULOUS teens before Stanford, I dreamed private, sensual dreams, conjuring up the man I would someday marry. My imaginary suitor never had a face, only dark, passionate eyes that consumed me with admiration and unspoken longing. His key trait, if not intensity, was surely unending kindness, for some part of me was searching for the ever-loving father I never had.

Among the qualities I sought in my unknown faceless lover, "oddball" had never made the list; it wasn't a trait that would even occur to a serious-minded girl.

Yet oddball was what I got.

I'D BEEN AT Stanford nearly a year when my life changed. I first saw Rob Wills at a summer get-acquainted dance euphemistically called a Jolly-Up. At eighteen I wasn't expecting much, since so far the campus men seemed to fall into two categories—the nerds or the party animals—and those who didn't spend our date lingering on the mysteries of subatomic particles, were inclined to squander it instead guffawing with friends over last weekend's drunken bash at Mama Risotti's. (Never mind that to those who held such hi-jinks in high esteem I was one of the nerds.)

To put it more accurately, Rob first saw me at the Jolly-Up and I never saw him at all. The flirting I did with the men observing from the sidelines had a kind of high-water mark, based on the fact that I'm tall, over five-ten, and resolutely never made eye contact with anyone shorter than six-foot-two, nor even noticed they were there. All my little smiles and coy glances went to the men who towered above the rest. It's faintly possible that sometime during the evening my eyes flicked across the top of Rob Wills's head, but I certainly never saw his face.

The truth was, I didn't know he existed until he cut in on me.

He introduced himself, and when he took my hand to begin dancing, I saw at once that he wasn't up to my height standards, his eyes being only slightly taller than mine, and when he looked at me it wasn't with anything close to desperate unspoken longing, but something nearer amusement. He seemed awfully tan, too, and more so because his teeth were so white. Furthermore, he didn't fit my physical ideal in other ways; instead of the comfortable, filled-out shape I'd envisioned, he was as skinny as a mop handle.

All in all, he didn't seem promising.

"I tried to catch your eye," he said as he guided me across the floor, "but your eye wasn't catchable."

That's a novel opening line. Having no fitting response, I fell back on a conventional tack and asked him to repeat his name, learning he was called, formally, Robert Victor Wills.

"Where are you from, Robert Victor Wills?"

"Call me Rob," he said. "Where am I from, you ask? You mean last week or last year?"

Once again he threw me, and being an intensely-bookish type in those days and absolutely no good at fast repartee, I was still fumbling for words when he grinned and said, "I'm from Hawaii."

Well, that explained everything: the dark skin (I learned later he tans if he walks past an open window) the gaudy aloha shirt, the owlish glasses. What the glasses had to do with such an assessment has now escaped me, but I said, "Oh, you're Hawaiian!"

"Not exactly," he said. "That's just where I lived last. I'm transferring back to Stanford from U of Hawaii. My dad's a Naval officer, so we traveled. Never stayed in one place long enough to tire of it." He smiled again, a generous smile that conveyed uncomplicated enthusiasm for his nomadic life. "How about you?"

"I grew up in lots of places, too. Los Angeles. Denver. Rochester, New York. A ranch in Mt. Shasta, California." Unlike him, I'd hated the moving around. "My dad's a doctor, but I've never lived with him. My mom divorced him when I was two. She's not your normal, everyday mother, she's sort of a Bohemian." *And she's been married seven times,* I thought, *which only my mom considers amusing.*

The music changed tempo and we danced faster. I was glad to see that the mop handle was graceful, that in spite of his shortness and not being an inch over six feet, I felt good dancing with him. When the piece was over he seemed reluctant to let me go, and instead pulled me off to one side and asked urgently, "Is anyone taking you home?"

"Yes."

"Who?"

I gaped at him, so surprised at his bluntness that all decent answers melted away. "You want to know his name?" Flustered, I suddenly couldn't remember the name myself.

"Never mind," he said. "I withdraw the question." And then an abrupt switch. "Do you like to swim?"

"You mean in a swimming pool or the ocean?"

"The ocean. It's the only swimming that counts. I used to be a surfer, learned how at Waikiki Beach." He gave me that smile again. "What are you doing tomorrow?"

Another blunt question; he was so full of them. *Well, that depends, I guess, on what you're offering.* Before I could figure out a way to hedge and be cool about it, he said, "How would you like to go to a beach party?"

"A beach party?" I was beginning to sound like a parrot, echoing every word he said, but I needed time to think and he never gave me any, he just kept peppering me with questions and throwing me off balance.

"That's right, at Santa Cruz beach. We'll go about eleven. You should come, it'll be fun, I promise." He said it with a smile, with conviction, as if there could be no doubt.

I guessed then he was a fraternity man and he'd waited until the dance to nail down a date. But he seemed pretty sure of himself, not at all concerned, and in fact all his words were positive and definitely self-assured. He was looking at me with an intensity that lent his thin face a kind of radiance. Rob Wills was awash in youthful energy and high spirits, but I doubted he'd be serious-minded enough, long run, or mature enough to interest me.

Still, one little date for the beach wasn't a lifetime commitment, and I thought, *What the heck.*

"I think I'm free," I said. "A beach party sounds fine, I'd love to go." In fact it sounded more than fine, because above all I'd heard the word "party," which meant I'd meet other men, some of whom would no doubt be taller and less frivolous and wouldn't ask blunt questions.

In due course I went back to my dorm with the somebody else, and whoever he was, he'd already become indistinct and shadowy, dimmed by the brightness of Rob Wills.

THE NEXT DAY everything changed.

When I went down to breakfast late, I found a note from Rob in my box—a note so strange and personal, so shocking, really, I squirmed as I began to read. After the first few sentences I ducked into a secluded corner of the lobby, convinced my embarrassed expression would give the contents away. "You remind me of someone I once loved," he began. "I was watching you at the dance, waiting for you to spot me, but you never did. You have wonderful legs, Maralys, and an aura that makes me feel I've known you forever."

Oh Lord, I'm not ready for this, it's too much. A love letter from a stranger. He was making me crazy, this maverick rolling through my life like an escaped tire, as blunt on paper as he was in person. Glancing around furtively to see who might be looking, I decided to get out of the lobby with the thing, lest it burst into flames.

Chagrined, I ran upstairs to talk to my roommate. "Listen to this note, Barbara. You won't believe it." She was wise and mature, thoughtful like I was, but quicker, with a tongue ten times faster than mine.

I read her all of it, or as much as I could endure. "In my room alone, I find myself unable to stop thinking about you. It's as though we've been on a collision course, destined forever to meet . . . "

She began to chuckle.

Toward the bottom of the page I had to stop, too embarrassed to go on. "He's got this image of me," I said. "He's put me on some kind of pedestal. Can you imagine, after three dances? What happens when reality sets in and I come clunking down to earth? What would you do, Barbara? How will I face him?"

"When is he picking you up?"

"In about half an hour . . ." A buzzer sounded in our room.

"Oh, Lord, that must be him!" I threw a look at the clock. "Can you believe this, he's early! And I'm not even dressed!"

"You'd better *get* dressed," said Barbara. "And wear plenty of clothes. I'm not sure I'd bring a bathing suit. Not with what he's thinking."

"But it wasn't a sexy note. It was all poetic allusions, his romantic notions of who I am."

"Where do you think sex starts?"

I ignored that; it was too much to get into. "And now I have to go down there, feeling like my soul is exposed."

She said dryly, "It's not your soul you should worry about."

ROB WILLS WAS leaning against a wall in the lobby, loose-legged and careless, smiling the way I remembered from the night before. But he surprised me again, because he didn't mention the note, nor did he seem the slightest bit awkward. "Did I rush you?" he asked pleasantly.

"Well . . . sort of. I wasn't quite ready." *I wasn't ready at all.* I couldn't face him, couldn't look him in the eyes. *Please don't ask about the note.* I had my swimsuit under my clothes, hoping I'd never have to take them off.

If Rob noticed my silence he didn't seem to care, but bounded across the lobby in high spirits, expecting me to follow. "Let's go. Our ride is waiting outside."

"Where are the others?"

He stopped. "What others?"

"You know . . ."

He obviously didn't know, and gave me a puzzled look, then pointed to the door. "It's out there," he said.

Second surprise: Our ride wasn't a "ride" at all, nor even close to what I'd expected. The transportation waiting for us outside was an aged green Model-A parked randomly to the curb. And the jalopy came with a driver—its owner. Rob's friend, if that's what he was, hovered near the car—a solemn-looking male, thin and desiccated, like an old leaf.

Rob introduced us with an offhanded gesture. "This is Hudson Bowlby," and Bowlby acknowledged me with bored eyes and the flattest of "hi's." No mention of friendship there, no hint of who he was. They couldn't be buddies, I thought, they were acting too distant, almost like strangers. Then why was he here?

"Get in," said Rob, and pointed to the ancient automobile's one narrow seat. Black, of course.

I climbed into the car gingerly and without enthusiasm. "Not much room," mumbled Bowlby, an unnecessary comment since I'd already noticed. Only inches were left for Rob, who squeezed in beside me.

Third surprise, revealed after a few pointed questions: everything I'd assumed the night before was wrong. Here, jammed together on the seat of a green Model-A, was the sum total of Rob's beach party—Maralys Klumpp, Robert Victor Wills, and Hudson Bowlby, all bound for Santa Cruz beach in Bowlby's geriatric car. And two out of three not exactly happy about it.

The car started with an asthmatic wheeze and clunked its way down Stanford's tree-lined Memorial Drive. I could hardly believe what I'd gotten myself into. "You mean nobody else is coming?" I asked for the second time. "Nobody's meeting us there?"

"No," said Rob. He seemed surprised I was still probing.

"This is what you call a *party?*"

"Sure," he said. "We're going to the beach, aren't we? I've brought some food. It's a party."

It's not what I call a party! "You're not a member of a fraternity?"

"No. Did I ever say I was?"

I looked over at him, so pleased with himself, so unruffled, so content with this idiotic arrangement, and I couldn't help smiling. "Do you always exaggerate like this?"

He smiled too, his eyes alive with merriment. "I never promised you anything else."

"No, I suppose you didn't. It's what you implied." *Your word choices,* I thought, *the way you asked, your voice. You created an illusion—and it was all false.* "What other surprises have you got in mind?"

He threw me a wait-and-see look.

Right then I realized he was even more unusual than I thought. And maybe a lot more fun, too.

After that, with Hudson Bowlby driving with his eyes straight ahead like the world's best-trained English chauffeur, Rob and I talked without stopping.

To my surprise, Rob was more than he'd seemed at first. A great deal more. Under his outer layer of wacky, offhanded nuttiness, was a different Rob, an intense, serious man. I saw at once that he was keenly aware of the world beyond Stanford, and brimming with insights.

The two of us quickly forgot Bowlby was there, and we went ahead and settled all the pressing world's problems between ourselves. We found we agreed on War, Sex, Money, Racial Discrimination, Peace, and Students Who Smoke—all more exhilarating than discovering we both hated sauerkraut.

(Some day I mean to look up Hudson Bowlby and ask him just what we did decide, since we don't agree on everything anymore. Somebody has shifted ground, and I'd like to review Money and Sex.)

Halfway there I glanced sideways and noticed Rob's strong, distinct profile and I thought, *That's a good face.* And then I thought, *What a mind he's got!* And right then I stopped caring that he needed to grow two more inches.

Once at Santa Cruz beach, we found the water too frigid for swimming, so we sat on the sand and went on talking. I could never remember, later, exactly what happened to Hudson Bowlby. I do remember asking, "How come you brought *him?*" and Rob answering, "We had to get to the beach, didn't we? Bowlby had the only car I could lay my hands on."

I stared at him—a man who knew how to get what he wanted—then broke into laughter because he was so outrageous.

After a while we ate the peanuts, cheesy crackers, candy bars and grape juice Rob had provided as food.

"I hope you own a bike," he said as Bowlby drove us home again, having reappeared from wherever he'd gone.

"I do, but it's old and doesn't go very fast."

"That's all right. As long as it works. We'll be able to get around, which is all that counts."

I WAS HAPPILY aware that I now had a close friend on campus—a friend who cared deeply about everything, who was neither a nerd nor a party animal—a friend who was male.

His brains were what did it, the ultimate appeal to an earnest, appallingly-sincere, non-small-talking egghead like me.

I hadn't thought it would happen.

Of course there was still the screwball side of him to contend with, the Rob who did *nothing* like anyone else. While other men summoned their dates from the dorm lobby via a buzzer, he stood under my third-floor window at Casa Ventura and whistled. The first three notes of the World War I battle song, "Over There," told me—and every girl on that side of the building—that Rob Wills and his bicycle had arrived. He knew they all heard him . . . as though he was whistling for his friend to come out and play . . . he knew but he simply didn't care.

When I looked down, he'd be staring up at my window expectantly, like an eager Tom Sawyer, with shower water still dripping off his brown hair.

It didn't bother him that other couples dated in cars. He was happy enough escorting me to the movies and around campus on his bicycle and mine.

FOR THE REST of the summer, the two of us were almost never apart. He had a friend take our picture with the bicycles near Casa Ventura. " . . . So we'll remember this summer," he said. "I believe in memorializing the things that count. Come on, babe, move a little closer."

It seemed Stanford had delivered, after all, the gift I never knew I wanted: Rob Wills.

No, more—months later it gave me an offbeat, unconventional, free-wheeling nut of a husband.

Early dates took Rob and Maralys to the beach.

Chapter Two

Riding to Glory

FOR THE REST of the summer, the courtship dipped in and out of our classes and ruined most of them. Scholastically, we came out bedraggled and besmirched. But as a couple we were doing fine.

When summer quarter was finally over, Rob asked me to go to Texas with him to visit his parents. "You'll like them, Babe," he said, with his old, beach-party enthusiasm. "Dad is smart—fairly serious but basically brainy, and my mom's a nut and really funny. Everyone likes her."

"I'd like to go with you, Rob." What I meant was, I'd like to go with you anywhere, to see your folks in Texas or the moon, but mainly I don't want our time together to end.

"We can take a train out of Los Angeles," he said, "but first we have to get to L.A." We looked at each other—two naïve students, newly in love. And then one of us said, "Let's hitchhike!" and the other said, "Why not?" as though the idea actually had a shred of merit. As though spontaneity was a virtue that deserved to be cherished above common sense.

Still, it wasn't common sense that threatened to scuttle our plan, but sheepishness. There we were, standing beside our suitcases on Bayshore Highway tentatively holding out our thumbs . . . in my case with the same dawning mortification I'd had years earlier when forced to admit to myself I would never fully grasp the logic behind long division. Here was a new way to feel demeaned.

I, who'd never hitchhiked before in my life, could barely get my thumb to point in the right direction. Dressed like other Stanford coeds of the day in skirt, sweater, pearls, and pumps, I fancied myself born to the gracious class, a notch or two above your usual hitchhiker.

But as cars disdainfully hurtled past offering nothing more than a windy aftermath, all that graciousness blew away. Pearls or no pearls, begging rides from strangers had its tacky side, like straightening your panties when no one's looking. My hand kept faltering and I had to keep pushing it out there, into the visual field of oncoming traffic. Finally I said, "Rob, I'm no good at this."

"It's not exactly my thing, either."

"What if the wrong people come along?"

He gazed at me, for once with no answer.

"How will the right people know we're the right people?"

"Maybe we can tell them," he said. He gave me one of his thoughtful looks and then, skinny and driven as he was, he took off running along the highway looking for something, though for what, I hadn't a clue. With Rob, ideas frequently weren't expressed out loud, but simply acted upon. Sometimes the deed would merely appear, done and finished and presented with a kind of "Voila!" . . . and it was assumed I'd be charmed.

He soon came back holding a big piece of blank cardboard. "We'll make a sign, babe. You got a pen in your purse?"

I didn't. But then I dug deeper. "How about this?"

"Excellent," he said. "Good thinking, Babe," and using my brilliant red lipstick, he consumed most of it printing the giant words, STANFORD TO LOS ANGELES.

"There . . ." holding up his sign for my scrutiny, "that says it all." I smiled. He didn't seem to require my approval, not seriously. It was obvious that this work of genius had arrived pre-approved.

Edging closer to the highway, he blended into his sign and became a billboard with legs. Billboards being nicer than hitchhikers,

I felt he'd given us a different aura, splashed us with new respectability. Any minute a genteel college professor would stop and whisk us away in his Oldsmobile.

Not for an instant did I imagine a different scenario, that we might be stepping, instead, into the twilight zone. With my usual optimism flowering away, I stood beside Rob and his sign, composing my face for innocence and trying to convey a message. *We may be hitchhiking, but we're not really hitchhikers, you understand, we're students, and this is beneath us.* A lot to convey in a split second.

Our sign's tour of duty was brief. In only minutes, an enormous truck with attached trailer abruptly veered off the highway, sending up plumes of dust as it pulled to a stop a block away. I wasn't even sure the eighteen-wheeler was stopping for us. But before I could comment, Rob had lifted his suitcase and started running toward the behemoth. I called after him, "Tell him thanks, Rob. Thanks anyway."

While I waited and watched from a distance, Rob and the driver exchanged words, and then Rob was running back to me.

"Did he take it okay?" I said, but to my horror he grabbed my suitcase. "Come on, Babe," he said cheerily.

For seconds I just stood there, stunned. "But Rob! That's a *truck*! We can't go in *that*!"

"He's giving us a ride," said Rob, as though this was a perfectly acceptable idea, as though this was the kind of transportation we accepted every day. "Come on. He's waiting."

"It's a truck!" I shrilled again, but he was leaving me, and suddenly I had a new and awful choice. Remain on the highway by myself or follow my boyfriend. The deserted island or the shark. With feet so slow they could hardly be construed as moving, I dragged down the shoulder toward Rob. This must have been the moment when I surrendered control of my destiny for all time.

As I reached the alien nether world of rumbling trucks and earthy truck drivers, the man was already deciding my fate. A burly fellow whose belly lapped over his belt, he was just tossing my suitcase up into the trailer, into some kind of void where it simply fell out of sight.

I watched it disappear. *Whither my case goest,* I thought glumly, *I will go also.*

The man pointed to the great metal steps. In my nice skirt (all women wore nice skirts back then), I was supposed to climb the three enormous steps and deposit my feminine self inside that yawning cab. Me, a Stanford girl who'd signed the honor code and actually believed in it. At heart an elitist, an intellectual snob. Make that a total snob. And here I was with two men who thought it not at all odd that I should enter the ultimate in a man's world and ride ingloriously in a *commercial truck!*

Still on the ground, I looked around. There was no escape, nowhere else to go.

Grabbing a handle of sorts, I pulled myself up and finally landed on a broad leather seat. Rob came up and plopped down beside me. I was stuck. Stuck, stuck, stuck.

The driver came around and started the engine and our world began to move. I could feel every ton of that truck, sense its tires bumping over the dirt and making their way back to solid pavement.

Perched unhappily between the two men, I soon perceived a further problem. Between me and the driver was a forest of gears, one handle after another, and as the man revved through the gears, we both quickly grasped that he had no place to shift except up my skirt. Making a fast adjustment, I pulled my legs out of the way. But then he needed another gear, and another, and the whole sequence became impossible. I didn't want his gears rubbing my legs, but then neither did he.

Within a block, the man was pulling over again so Rob and I could change places. So now Rob was in the middle and I sat next to the dust-coated window. Right outside the glass, the exhaust pipe belched and roared and filled my right ear with thunderous noise. From then on I could hear little of what was being said.

However, from time to time Rob shouted bits of information in my direction, which is how I learned that our driver's name was

Frank, and that his cargo consisted of ten tons of sugar. While the men talked, I sat there feeling more and more like a bug sucked toward a drain.

But that wasn't the worst of it. We'd only been on the road an hour, bumping and careening down the highway, when another giant truck-and-trailer swung around us, accidentally veered off the highway in front of us and ran down the shoulder, raising a tornado of boiling dust . . . into which we drove at full speed with zero visibility.

I was aghast—both for the other truck and for us. In my head I was screaming, "Slow down, Frank!" but no words came out.

Rob turned to look at our driver, but strangely, Frank seemed unconcerned. He sat there gripping the wheel, staring ahead into the dust, nodding as the runaway rig regained the pavement. The dust cleared and we were still on the road, even in our own lane, and the incident seemed over.

Except it wasn't.

Minutes later, our own rig accelerated, swung out to overtake the other truck, pulled hard into the right lane and veered toward the edge. In seconds we, too, were off the pavement, bumping crazily down the dirt, wholly out of control and lurching from side to side.

I was so terrified I felt myself turning white. With no seatbelt for security, I grabbed the dashboard and held on, sure we were about to strike a tree or a ditch, knowing we were seconds from death. The truck careened downhill, as reckless as a truck could get, hurtling the three of us toward eternity. For someone who adores all things sweet it seemed ironic that I was about to die under a runaway mountain of sugar. In my head I was screaming at Rob: *I told you this was a terrible idea!*

After what felt like hours, but must have been only a minute, Frank ended the horrifying ordeal and brought us back to pavement—back to some marginal kind of safety.

Releasing my grip on the dashboard, I turned to stare at the man behind the wheel.

He was laughing. "I guess I got *him!*" he chortled, and with a glance in the side mirror, I saw behind us a cloud of dust obscuring the road. Clearly the other truck was now plunging ahead as we'd done earlier, driving blind.

"I really dusted him!" shouted Frank for our amusement . . . except Rob didn't look amused, and I was so *unamused* I wanted only to order that idiot man to stop the rig and let me out. Actually, I yearned to throttle him where he sat.

But neither could work . . . the first because we were miles from anywhere.

I waited for Rob to do something. Glancing sideways, I saw his irritation and wondered that he didn't speak up and tell the driver to drop us off at the next town. But he didn't, and it was clear that Rob had chosen this singular mode of travel and now meant to stick with it. I wasn't sure whether "sticking it out" was a good character trait or bad.

The rest of the night was long. Entertaining us further, our man gleefully exhumed stories about runaway trailers that overran their cabs and sliced through their driver's compartments, instantly killing them. He told heartwarming tales of trucks losing their brakes on the steep, winding Grapevine and accelerating out of control down the endless grade, unable to make the required turns, unable to find an escape ramp in time.

At moments he actually made Rob laugh. But not for one second did I ever find him funny.

I wasn't sure why he'd picked us up. But finally he revealed his motive: we were there to keep him *awake!*

With such a driver, there was no danger any of us would sleep. The rest of the night I sat stiff as a tree trunk, and when we began barreling down the Grapevine, I watched each curve intently, judging the sharpness of the turn, waiting for the awful acceleration to begin.

True to the last of my nerdish instincts, I monitored our driver with my own set of standards, the Stanford Debutante Test of Acceptability, and on one of the steeper grades it became obvious our man was not driving at prudent speeds, and in fact the truck had picked up so much wild and dangerous momentum, the driver should be searching for an escape ramp. Any fool could feel the straining of the brakes and sense the trailer's urgent impulses to overtake the cab. Reaching for the dashboard, I held on, consumed by terror. *Oh dear God! Here comes the sugar!*

Miraculously, though we flew by an escape ramp, the truck held together and the trailer did not come forward to pay us an unexpected visit.

As the truck finally roared down the last hill and slowed in Los Angeles, light was just creeping up behind the hills. Rob and I got out and for seconds stamped our feet, wondering if we could walk. Before we left, I actually thanked our driver—out of sheer gratitude that we were still alive.

With that event, our hitchhiking ended forever.

But my life with Rob went on. When I looked back on our early months together, I thought of that trip—the hitchhiking part—as a defining moment, an occasion that caught the spirit of our relationship. Because of Rob I did the unthinkable, pitted my girlish, delicate self against a truck, and somehow came out a winner.

In later years, I would experience something similar with my oldest son, and I would feel that sense of triumph once again. You always win when you take on an experience that lasts in your memory forever.

CHAPTER THREE

Mrs. Brittell's Back Porch

ROB'S PARENTS WERE exactly as he'd said: his father, Art, gentlemanly and serious—balanced by Ruth, as vivacious and fluttery as a butterfly. Impossible not to like her.

The next month, Rob and I slid out of Stanford quietly, without fuss or fanfare. It was all too unnoticed, too unheralded.

A prideful, bookwormish student like me doesn't leave a school like Stanford without a backward glance, so I was obviously not thinking clearly, but what did I know then . . . only nineteen and ripe to get married, following the lead of someone so brainy and fascinating I couldn't imagine my life moving forward without him.

Our leaving took place by degrees—first Rob, then me.

How was he to know that the summer he chose to take two killer science courses—Qualitative Analysis and Organic Chemistry, both condensed (each a year's work crammed into one quarter), he'd also meet me? His grades slipped and Stanford put him on probation. "Go down to San Jose State," they said, "bring up your grades, and come back."

His pride was seriously stung. "I'll transfer all right . . . " he said it with a certain grimness, a subtle set to the jaw that I would later see as one of his trademarks, "but I'm not coming back."

I was only beginning to recognize the hard metal stratum that lay beneath his mercurial outer self.

A few weeks later we were in separate schools, divided by a length of Bayshore Highway and a forty-minute commute in Rob's newly acquired but almost prehistoric roadster, a munge-green Lafayette dubbed the Turtle because of its low-slung, stumpy-looking rear end.

"This drive is hell on wheels," he said after a few weeks, "it's getting more grinding by the day. And where do I fit in homework? Nowhere, at the moment. Changes must be made. I've got to study more and see you less."

"See me less? But Rob . . ."

Which explains why, at the start of winter quarter, I left my precious ivy-league school to join him at San Jose State.

ROB HAD BEEN renting a tiny student room—a converted porch is all it was—from a Mrs. Brittell. To understand why we spent our first married month living on Mrs. Brittell's back porch, you'd have to know that we'd left ourselves only one week between quarters to apply for a marriage license, a college transfer, an admission to San Jose State, a wedding ring and a Wasserman Test—though not necessarily in that order—and there simply wasn't time to look for an apartment too.

Nor was there time to put together a decent wedding—or, for that matter, any wedding at all.

Since we're both terribly romantic—Rob doesn't admit to this, but he gets misty-eyed in certain movies—the idea of being married in a judge's downtown office began to give the pair of us a bleak, sagging feeling. As we waited to meet the judge, I looked around his forbidding office—no carpets, small windows, and a lot of dark wooden furniture that would have added layers of dreariness to an office in Tombstone—and I nudged Rob and whispered, "Honey, we can't be married here!"

Rob nodded. "It's not exactly a church."

"Ask him if we can't do it tonight—in his living room."

With proper deference, Rob broached the subject, and the judge looked up and shrugged. His face had no more life than his office. "Doesn't make any difference to me. You can come over if you want to." He scribbled on a piece of paper. "Here's the address. Do you have any witnesses?"

"No."

"I'll provide a couple."

That night we learned a useless lesson—useless because we'd never need it again: if you want a romantic wedding in a judge's home, you'd better pick a romantic judge.

We arrived at his home at seven, both of us so slicked up and nervous it was almost like having a real wedding after all. We'd been thinking about the prospect all week—*we* were getting *married*—and it was beginning to feel like a serious, grownup step. Driving over there I even dared hope that the judge's wife might get into the spirit and provide some small touch, like candles, or a slice of cake . . . a simple gift, perhaps . . . anything to add formality and romance to the occasion. But I didn't mention this to Rob, because in case she didn't, he might be disappointed.

The judge ushered us into his dining room and pointed to one side of a modest table. Starched and unsmiling, or just naturally bored, he positioned himself on the other side, and his young son, about eleven, came out just then and stood stiffly beside him and the father began to intone the ceremony. I looked around. Where was the wife? Would she appear in time to be a witness? Was this even legal?

No, apparently she wouldn't appear (and I hope no one ever presses us on the legality), because she obviously had a higher calling in the kitchen. We knew she was busy because we could hear her, as sounds of running water and clacking dishes and other homey noises kept coming and going during our nuptials. Mind you, they didn't take long. The judge must have found an abbreviated version, skipping such trivials as "for better or for worse, in sickness and in health," and proceeding directly to the "I now pronounce you . . . " which saved him significant amounts of time but left us with skimpy, pared-to-the-bones vows.

But I felt lucky anyway—partly because I was marrying Rob, and partly because he looked so awed and serious he made the ceremony resonate with significance right through the clatter from the kitchen. After a while I forgot everything except the expression in his eyes. When it was over, a look of profound tenderness came over his face, and he pulled me close and kissed me. He seemed to be saying he *meant* all the vows of marriage, even the ones the judge had skipped.

My heart melted. We hadn't needed a cake or candles or a present after all. Rob made it an eloquent wedding all by himself.

Now, years later, I've almost forgiven the judge's wife, since it's possible her husband forgot to mention he'd be marrying two people right after dinner and please cushion the noise from the kitchen.

We went to a hotel that night, and the next day, after I'd finished registering at San Jose State, I asked brightly, "Well, honey. Where are we going to live?"

He looked surprised. "In my room, of course."

"*Your room?* Are you serious? You mentioned something yesterday but I thought you were kidding."

"I do have a bed in there."

"Uh, yeah—I guess you do. But Rob, it's so . . . tiny. And what about my clothes?"

"We'll run up to Stanford this afternoon and collect your stuff," he said, missing the point.

Even Mrs. Brittell seemed taken aback when Rob walked up to her front door asking permission with his arms full of my suitcases. "Well, I suppose you can both stay in that room," she said, hesitating, "if you think you can manage. But the bed's pretty small . . . " She looked dubious. "It's all right with me, I guess." It was plain she thought there was no accounting for newlyweds.

With one of his charming smiles, Rob thanked her, and now, having solved our housing problem, he led the way around to the back of the house and up the narrow steps to the enclosed porch. The room was about six by nine. He went in and plunked down all the suitcases, then turned to me. "Well—here we are!" It was the same exuberance, the same blind delight he'd had in Hudson Bowlby's arthritic Model A.

I followed, and barely able to get into the room with both Rob and the luggage already inside, I smiled and echoed with no enthusiasm at all, "Right. Here we are."

"Let me get these things out of the way." Rob attempted to shove the cases under the bed, but the bed was too low and too narrow, and they didn't come close to fitting. "Guess we'll have to lay them flat on the floor, then," he said, and while I perched on the bed he spread the suitcases end to end and they filled the entire open space. From then on, we walked across my imitation alligator bags to get in and out.

It wasn't so bad having a floor made of inlaid suitcases, but we did miss the presence of a desk. Since the bed was the room's only raised surface, it eventually served as study table, barber's chair, dinette, and—when we were tired enough—a bed. But first we had to toss our books over onto the luggage and brush the cookie crumbs onto the books.

To say we "slept" in the bed would be a euphemism. It wasn't a bed, anyway, it was a cot, and though we spent plenty of hours there, we extracted about as much genuine rest as two large people could expect from a narrow padded plank. It was barely possible for both of us to lie on the cot stacked on edge, like two phonograph records.

At first Rob thought it was wonderful. Cozy. "You're so soft, Babe," he murmured from time to time, giving me a little squeeze. "Isn't it nice to be married?"

"Heavenly," I said, while circulation slowly backed up in my right leg, which was mashed against the wall. "Though I didn't think marriage would be quite so crowded. I'd like a little more room to be married in."

"Room?" he sounded almost hurt. "What do we need more room for? We're so *close* this way," pulling me still closer.

Then we began getting tired. Rob cautioned, "Now look, Babe, don't try to straighten your legs. I like to sleep with my legs bent, and if we're going to stay aboard a bed this small we have to be shaped the same."

"But I don't like sleeping with bent legs—not all the time. Let's straighten them once in awhile."

We began disagreeing as we slept. Since Rob was in charge of nocturnal maneuvers, when he wanted to turn, we both turned. But occasionally I was in the middle of some nice dream that didn't require a change, and when he went into one of those authoritative shifts, I resisted. Whereupon he jerked the covers until he was rolled up in them like a sausage and I was left blinking and wide awake. Also cold. I'd grab the covers back, and *he'd* wake up. If this happened several times in one night, we fought in the daytime, too. In those days I wasn't used to following orders in my sleep.

This went on for several weeks until one day when Rob was in class and I wasn't, I sneaked out and rented a brand new apartment. It felt like a bold move, as though I'd emancipated myself and gone off to Washington on a bra-less march, and I was afraid Rob would be angry, but he was delighted. "I'm glad you did that, Babe. Cozy is cozy, but enough is enough."

We said good-bye to Mrs. Brittell, who, as a parting token of affection, sent us off with her old washing machine.

Soon my mother sent down a truckload of furniture from her ranch in Mt. Shasta, and included were some nice things, like a brown Bigelow rug, plus a few old formal chairs of the not-too-sturdy type, that collapsed into splinters under our weightier friends.

Then there was a big black sleigh bed—a veritable monster of a bed—but a thing of beauty, I thought, compared to the cot at Brittell's. It was so very *substantial.*

"You know, it's not that bad looking," I said as we were struggling to put it together. "It has a homey look—kind of comfortable and old fashioned."

"That's one way to describe it," Rob said, grimacing as he tried to ram an eight inch bolt into a rail.

"I mean, there's something special about an antique."

"Yeah, there is. It's especially *old.*" He pounded the bolt all the way in while I held the rail in place. "There," he said at last, straightening up. "That should take care of it."

"You see?" I said, looking at the two curled ends, quite expansive and very black. "It's really rather handsome, isn't it?"

Rob studied the bed dubiously and finally came up with the only compliment he could muster. "I suppose you could say it has some kind of old world charm."

The bed was listening.

One morning at two A.M. Old World Charm dumped us on the floor. Well, actually, it dumped us on the floor from the waist down. One minute we were sound asleep and the next our legs were bent at the waist and falling precipitously. Crash! The end rail hit the floor and the mattress jarred to a stop.

"What happened? What happened?" I shrieked, wide awake instantly. I thought we'd had an earthquake.

"Damn bed," Rob growled.

"That was *the bed*?" The crash of the rail echoed in my ears and I could still feel the sensation of falling.

"Damn rotten, poorly-made bed," Rob muttered. We were too shocked to move. Our feet were sloped dramatically downhill, and we were gripping the top of the mattress like two people clinging to a wisp of bush on a steep mountainside. Purely instinctive, as even a bird doesn't want to be thrown out of the nest.

"No good, flimsy weak bed," said Rob, at an uncomfortable tilt from which he was still not moving.

"What happened?" I asked for the third time.

"It collapsed. Hell, I don't know what happened, our bed's on the floor, that's all."

Well, so it was. Eventually, since we had to get back to sleep, we disentangled ourselves from the covers and climbed off the sloping mattress to begin the resurrection. Rob went into the kitchen for a hammer and screwdriver, and I stood by and tried not to seem in any way offensive, lest I be lumped in the same category as the bed.

Rob lifted the foot end saying crossly, "Here!" and I held everything suspended while he pounded and screw-drivered down under. After more cursing and a considerable amount of time, Rob finally had it fixed and we got back in. But now we couldn't sleep, so we spent the rest of the night giggling, because once the shock had worn off there *was* something funny about a collapsing bed.

A week later it happened again. Another crash and we were down, every bit as mad as the first time, but even more surprised, because we really thought Rob had made the necessary repairs. This time we didn't lie around expecting our problem to go away.

He jumped to the floor calling the bed a son-of-a-something a bed could never be the son of, adding that fixing beds ranked extremely low in a list of best things to do at one a.m., and further directing me to "get out of that weak-boned piece of furniture and grab this end!"

Now I was sorry, apologetic, even, that I'd ever had a nice word for the bed. Right then I wished to retract whatever praise I'd uttered for something so mean-spirited . . . and yes, ugly.

Over the months I began to notice the bed was a thick, stubborn lump, so monstrously heavy it wouldn't budge an inch if Rob tried to move it one way or another, but it moved plenty when it felt like it.

For as long as we lived in that apartment, and for its own temperamental reasons, the black sleigh threw us to the floor periodically, always at strange intervals, and generally just as we'd grown to trust it again. Old World Charm was like a horse with a bad temper—deceptively docile on its better days. But you just couldn't predict its moods, so you never knew when it was going to turn mean and eject you.

Usually we cursed and dragged ourselves out of the covers, but there came a night when we were just too tired, and instead of getting to his feet, Rob growled, "Oh, the hell with it . . ." and we slept at a jaunty tilt for the rest of the night.

The next day Rob surveyed the remains of our black sleigh spread across the floor. "Be sure to write your Mother and thank her for this lovely antique!"

The bed wasn't the only distinctive personality that shared our apartment. There was also Mrs. Brittell's washing machine, a solid Clydesdale by nature, as doughty and reliable as our bed was unreliable, and in addition, a marvel of Thirties engineering. Neither Rob nor I have ever seen another like it. The machine was approximately the age of our flighty bed, but had a determined spirit and a warm, giving heart—and it did its job with undaunted energy. Shaped like a great iron cradle, it sat on our back porch and rocked violently back and forth, while clothes, soap, and water gathered in frothy tidal waves and heaved from one side to the other.

There were no subtleties about the machine—it neither rinsed, wrung, nor spun, all that was up to us—but it certainly did *wash* . . . and it could have taught our bed a lesson in fidelity.

The washing machine became our resident comic performer. Since Rob and I had never seen an appliance with such an odd shape and so much vigor, we used to run it just for our amusement, and sometimes we fired it up to entertain friends.

"Come see what's on our back porch," we said, "if you want to meet the real character in this apartment."

But we didn't take it with us when we finally left San Jose, partly because of its mammoth weight, and partly because neither of us believed its plucky old heart could last much longer.

TOGETHER, ROB AND I finished the school year at San Jose State, where we'd signed up jointly for child psychology and genetics. All I remember about those courses, besides the fact that we were both finally studying and consequently earning stunning grades, is that Rob and I bred a lot of fruit flies, which kept waking prematurely from their anesthetized state and escaping into the classroom, where they bred surreptitiously with other students' flies and ruined everyone's experiments.

ROB WAS THE prime mover behind our transfer to UCLA. "Let's go back to Stanford," I said, but his jaw got that look and I knew it was hopeless. Women who aren't married to flinty husbands say things like, "You should have made him go," but frankly, I'd just acquired this man and wasn't ready to push him to an ultimate test.

So we transferred to UCLA, instead of some other large school, for a reason that now seems flimsier than dust. "The surfing's terrific down in Los Angeles," Rob exclaimed, and he wore that same bright expression and exuded the same air of breathless excitement that once made me imagine a "beach party" would consist of a significant number of people gathered on the beach.

"Babe," he exulted, "the sand everywhere is broad and clean. And the water's warm," and then he added as an afterthought, "and UCLA's an excellent school."

His last statement was true. The rest wasn't.

Before long I learned that the Santa Monica version of the Pacific Ocean was only slightly warmer than the water that lapped across the shore at Santa Cruz, which, by the temperature registered on my toes and legs, left it pretty frosty as oceans go.

But that never mattered much.

We were soon so busy with all the homework piled on us by UCLA . . . and making new friends . . . and coping with the nausea that accompanied my first pregnancy . . . that we hardly ever saw the beach.

ROB AND I didn't realize it then, but our move south was the first of dozens of paradoxes that followed us through life, accompanying the various choices we made over the years. In fact, if someone asked me, "What is one of the inevitable consequences of living?" I'd say Irony.

Chapter Four

One Up on Mr. Blandings

UCLA WASN'T STANFORD—no school was Stanford except Stanford—but it was okay, because I was there with Rob. After awhile the school began to soften and feel comfortable and even "fit" like an old pair of jeans. What wasn't okay was where we lived, especially now that I was newly pregnant and had morning sickness, a horse-and-buggy misnomer that stands for day-long nausea, which only fades as your head hits the pillow and your stomach goes to sleep and drifts out of reach of the churning swells.

Our "home" was not a home, but a dingy apartment in a brown stucco building in downtown Santa Monica, designed not around central air but central odor. The place reeked. As we entered the building after school, a familiar smell hit us, as though the tenants were cooking some abominable mix of brussels sprouts and cabbage. I found myself breathing shallowly and longing for open windows. Rob wrinkled his nose and said, "Cabbage again?" and I wondered aloud whether it was the same family boiling new vegetables every day, or different families rotating through the same stinky menu. Never mind. The answer was unimportant; in my queasy state, daily contentment was impossible, living as we were among the fumes of simmering garbage.

Even without its odors, the apartment building was charmless:

the halls were dark enough for a mole and the wall paint older than the carvings on a Mayan temple.

One Saturday Rob and I went for a drive, looped up over a small mountain and came down again on a winding road, and, Voila!, we discovered the San Fernando Valley.

THE VALLEY WAS just over the hill from UCLA. It was a honeymooner's dreamscape abloom with freshly minted tract homes and opportunistic contractors charging around old cow pastures with blueprints under their arms. Dairies had once abounded there. Now everything above the well-fertilized soil was new, and even the sun shone brighter. It all looked so promising.

For not much money, which—with a Cal-Vet loan and help from our parents—was all we had, we could swing a brand new house and escape those malignant cooking odors.

"WE'LL TAKE THAT one," Rob and I chorused as our newly-chosen contractor, handsome Mr. Young of Young, Rosenberg and Spiegel, unfurled a sheet of sketches. We were looking at four renditions of an 850-square-foot house: two bedrooms, a bath, a kitchen, a living-room, and a dining nook. A mansion, really. Every sketch was basically the same house except for subtle differences (huge differences we thought), in windows or doors. But just claiming one of them as ours was like staking out a beachfront in Carmel-by-the-Sea. Rob and I pored over the sketches, examining them minutely as though they contained intricacies worthy of Hearst Castle.

Privately, the two of us slipped each other proud smiles, and then we signed important papers and wrote a big check for all the money we possessed, which was somewhere around two hundred dollars.

The house came with its own rectangle of earth, and that, too, was ours! As laid out on a flat piece of paper, the project seemed ideal. "Perfect, don't you think, Rob?" and he said, "Of course it's perfect—couldn't be better!" I was thinking how this topped our first car, even my first wrist watch, which I still remembered—the thrill of Mickey Mouse and his white-gloved finger, and how I felt *so old* wearing that watch at age six.

AS YOUNGISH ADULTS with limited life experience, Rob and I knew not the ways of contractors. We were innocently unaware of how some of them operated, or from what shadowy sources they drew the men who did the actual work—some of which we were about to find out.

Now that we'd signed the papers, the newly poured foundation drew us so irresistibly we couldn't stay away. Our chateau in the San Fernando Valley soon became Rob's personal challenge. I was growing a baby, but he was growing a *house.*

At first the place shaped up quickly, like a ripening plum. Exulting in its progress, Rob drove us out to the Valley every day after school just to look. The framing went up so fast we knew we'd have the home sooner than its due date. Much sooner. Which dovetailed perfectly with all the people who took one look at my generous stomach and asked, "Oh, are you due next month?"

One afternoon Rob walked across the cement, squeezed between a couple of two-by-fours and did a double-take. "Hey, what's this? There's supposed to be a door here!"

"You sure, Rob?"

"Sure I'm sure. I'm standing in the kitchen. I'm looking toward the garage. How are we supposed to get from one to the other?"

I eased in beside him. "How could they forget something as big as a . . . door?"

"Can't imagine. We'll have to find Mr. Young."

Full of purpose and youth, we sprinted down the row of half-framed houses and finally located Mr. Young. "You say they left out a door?" he asked pleasantly. "Well, that's a new one. I'll have to tell Mr. Rosenberg."

As it turned out, missing doors were new only to us. Days later the framers misplaced a window in the living room. "It's three feet off center," Rob explained patiently to Mr. Young, whom he'd found with some difficulty. "It's butted right up against the front door."

"Can't have that," said Young. "I'll see that Mr. Rosenberg gets on it immediately."

But Rosenberg didn't get on it—not until the lathers had covered up the frame. Rob marched up to the blank lathe and with a heavy, felt-tipped pen wrote "WINDOW HERE!" Still not satisfied, he drew the outline of a window in bold, thick strokes. Later, someone was sent to rip out half the living-room wall and re-locate the missing aperture.

Rob is nothing if not a man with audacious penmanship. I began to see his oversized words sprouting like modern-art daisies in all parts of the house.

Oddly, to the builders—to Mr. Young—Rob appeared monkishly calm. Aware of Rob's prickly impatience at home, how his temper sometimes flared like a sudden summer storm, I marveled that he was staying cool.

As the mistakes multiplied, Rob began to make lists, with letters big enough for the blind, which he handed to Mr. Young. Young accepted the lists agreeably and put them in his pocket, and we could only surmise that Mrs. Young ran the pockets through the washing machine with Rob's lists still in them.

Farther down the line, things got worse. Rob caught the flooring man hiking toward our bathroom with someone else's roll of linoleum slung over his shoulder. The cabinet-maker banged away in the kitchen framing out the wrong kitchen sink. And later he found the concrete man down on his knees busily forming the wrong patio. Still Rob never spoke of abandoning those contractors, and none of them saw the summer storm.

"This place is like a baby bird," Rob said, with a hint of affection. "We can't leave it alone for a minute."

"What do you suppose Young, Rosenberg and Spiegel *did* before they became contractors?"

He thought about it. "Nothing important. I can't picture them anywhere . . . even box boys would know the watermelon doesn't go on top of the bread."

OUR PLACE DID not arrive on time (any more than our first baby). By the end, its creation had slowed to such a crawl that it was two months late and we weren't given the keys until four days before Christmas.

Before we unloaded our few treasures at the new house, I ran inside to get a drink—and found no water coming from the faucets. Then I flipped a switch in the kitchen and discovered we had no electricity. Rob said evenly, "I suppose there's no heat in the floor furnace, either."

And there wasn't.

He looked around the living room and began to laugh. "Smile, Babe," he said, pulling me close and pointing. "Look over there. We're on *Candid Camera.*" I honestly thought he'd seen Allen Funt.

He turned serious. "Tonight there's going to be a cold snap," he said, and I asked how he knew.

"Heard it on the car radio. They're warning the citrus growers to fire up their smudge pots."

"Oh," I said. I was thinking about how we had no heat for the cold snap and no hot water. But then I remembered we had no water of any kind, either hot or cold.

I began feeling nostalgic about our apartment. It may have smelled of cabbage, but at least it was warm cabbage. And the place had water, too, of both varieties. I said, "What should we do?"

Rob threw a look at our non-functioning floor furnace and said with a grim smile, "I could always go out and buy a smudge pot."

That evening, as he held a flashlight and we lowered ourselves to a bare mattress, I said, "Honey, do you realize this is our first night living in our very first house?" My voice hit the bare walls and echoed back, as in a cave.

"What you mean is, it's our first night *camping* in our first house. Living is when you can turn on a light and flush a toilet."

"Well," I said, always the keeper of the flame of optimism, "at least there aren't any ants or mosquitoes."

"I'll grant you that, Babe." He laughed ironically and pulled me closer. "It's too cold for ants and you can't have mosquitoes without water."

ROB TOOK OVER. Naturally, we had no phone, either, a service that could only be obtained in the exploding frontiers of the San Fernando Valley by submitting a sob story worthy of *Queen for a Day:* "My husband has 2 broken legs and he's stuck on a ten-story roof. I'm waiting for a call from a crane company."

Which meant Rob spent every minute until Christmas down at the corner phone booth, pumping nickels into a slot as he tried to score a few basics, like water.

Each problem came with its own excuse: some idiot who thought he understood tractors had graded the front yard and torn out the water pipe; three idiots who considered themselves contractors had neglected to obtain any of the final inspections; an idiot in a cowboy hat who imagined he was an electrician had failed to bring the bathroom heater up to code. Having floundered in their pretenses, they all walked away.

Using his head and an endless supply of nickels, Rob turned contractor and slowly made things right.

By Friday night, the night before Christmas Eve, peace of a sort had come to Lindley Avenue. The furnace was now working, water came through the pipes, and we were the proud owners of a single strand of electricity . . . albeit from the contractor's power pole. Our mattress was still on the floor, but the floor was *warm.* "Just think," I murmured to Rob, "tomorrow we can take a bath."

TOMORROW CAME, BUT not the bath. Christmas eve morning we awoke to the sound of something large, an engine of some sort moving back and forth just outside our bedroom window. And then the doorbell rang. A man from the water company stood there asking if I knew we'd sprung a leak.

"A leak!" I howled, looking past his shoulder. In our front yard, a thin stream of water was shooting ten feet into the air. "That's not a leak. It's a geyser!"

"What happened?" he asked accusingly, as if he thought I'd been out there hacking at the pipe in my pajamas.

"No idea," I said. "We were asleep."

"I'll have to shut the water off."

"I suppose so." After all, we'd had water for eleven hours now, probably our quota for the year. Too bad so much of it disappeared in the ground.

Rob appeared at the door, watching as the geyser slowly receded. "You should see what else this one-man wrecking crew has done." He ran off to get his pants.

The wrecking crew was in our backyard. About seventeen years old, pimply and male, the lad was sitting atop a small yellow tractor, now stopped, blandly surveying our yard. Here, I realized, was one of the culprits . . . foolishly hired by Rosenberg to grade our lot. It was evident that Rob had already expressed a few opinions out the bedroom window, but also clear that the youth was a bit simple and didn't comprehend what all the fuss was about.

I stared at the kid curiously, wondering how his mind worked—or whether it worked at all—and how he'd managed to find and relentlessly destroy our underground plumbing. Not once, it seemed, but twice.

Rob gestured toward the front of the house. "*Why* . . ." he asked with exasperation he couldn't conceal, "didn't you stop when all the water broke loose?"

The boy looked at him blankly and said nothing.

"He sets off a geyser bigger than Yellowstone and he doesn't even notice," said Rob under his breath. "And why did you bury all this stuff I had piled up next to the house? Did you think we *wanted* cement bags and lathing mesh planted in our lawn?" So much stupidity, Rob seemed to think, must have a *reason.*

He was talking to the wrong person. I wasn't sure the kid was even listening.

"And that's not all," Rob said to me, because I was the only one paying attention. "Look over there—in the corner."

I looked. There was our power line dangling loose—our precious source of electricity doing a little dance in the corner of the yard.

"Why wasn't he electrocuted?"

Since the boy had had nothing to say so far, not even a comment as to how he'd managed to plow through 120 volts and live, there seemed no point in pushing him further.

Seeing that Rob and I had lapsed into disgruntled silence, the kid abruptly turned on the engine of his tractor. One could almost see him thinking, *Well, if they're through yapping at me, I guess I'll finish.*

Rob came to life and leaped in front of the tractor. "Oh no!" he said. "No you don't! You're not running that machine one more time. You're staying right here until I find Mr. Young." And with that he trekked off to the phone booth for the ninety-ninth time in four days.

To our surprise and relief, Mr. Young dragged himself away from a holiday party to attend to our problems—but only momentarily. He instructed the *kid* to find us a plumber, and while he also dredged up another electric wire, he left *Rob* to install it.

Neither was successful.

The kid wasn't able to locate a plumber on Christmas Eve, and after an hour's work Rob discovered the replacement wire was no good.

Also, during the afternoon the garage door blew shut on three of Rob's fingers, and his yelp was so bloodcurdling I thought he'd been electrocuted and the house had done us in at last.

I raced outside to find Rob hopping around over his smashed fingers, and was so relieved to see him still alive I screamed, "Oh, thank God!" much to his surprise.

Meanwhile, the kid—still plumberless at 4:00 P.M.—brought his father to our front yard, and the two of them knelt in the mud and wrestled with the broken water pipe. I was overjoyed to see them, especially the father.

Ultimately the two made a union of sorts and, lacking pipe joint compound, painted the union with red paint.

For non-plumbers it was quite an achievement, and Rob and I ran to the bathroom to test this latest plumbing job. To our surprise, when Rob turned on the water it came through red. For a moment we just stood there, looking.

And then I started cracking up—I couldn't help it—and so did Rob, both of us laughing hysterically, because what else could you expect after such a debacle but red water?

I can't recall exactly how we resolved all this. I do know that Rob found another electrical wire, and this one was good. Also, after it ran awhile, the water came through clear.

Since the banks, unaware of our disasters, had rudely closed early, leaving us penniless over the holidays, the tract salesman kindly lent us ten dollars. That night at 10:30 we found a haunted Christmas tree lot on Ventura Boulevard and bought a huge aromatic spruce for fifty cents and decorated it until three in the morning with popcorn and a few ornaments shipped to us by my mother. Somehow we felt entirely at peace because, after all, this was our first Christmas in our first, our very own home.

THE DAY AFTER Christmas, Monday morning early, a familiar sound broke into our dreams. A tractor!

In disbelief, we jerked awake to the ominous growl, the approaching and receding across the backyard.

This time we didn't lie in bed until the kid had run it through the house. Rob shot off the mattress and was outside in seconds, waving his arms like someone trying to flag down a train.

The kid stopped scooping building scraps into our flowerbeds and turned off the engine. Rob walked up to him and pointed toward the road. "Take that machine away—and don't ever come back!"

The last we saw of him, our lad was in the empty field across the street having a race *on the tractor* with a friend in a hot rod.

IN SPITE OF Young, Rosenberg, and Spiegel, Rob made his house come out all right.

After weeks of negotiation and a masterful letter from Rob, we settled the bill. In essence, Rob obtained their agreement that *they* pay for *their* mistakes.

ULTIMATELY, THE INFLUENCE of Young, Rosenberg and Spiegel on our lives was profound. Because of what they did for us—or rather, *to us*—our next forty-five years were markedly different than they might otherwise have been.

After Rob wrote them his summing-up letter, he gave it to me to read. He was outside lying on his back under the car when I finished the last page. Only his shoes were visible.

I was so excited I couldn't wait, and rushed up to the car and yelled down at his feet, "This letter is fantastic, Rob! It's great!"

"Yeah?" I could hardly hear his muffled response.

"I thought you'd blast those guys, I thought you'd pulverize them, but you didn't. Your letter is calm. It's rational. It says everything you needed to say. And every sentence is important."

His answer was garbled.

"Rob!" I cried, waving the letter excitedly as I made my final point to his shoes. "You should be a lawyer!"

Until then, he'd been getting a master's degree in psychometrics.

That letter changed his life.

And so, thanks to Young, Rosenberg and Spiegel, Rob did what nature and nurture intended him to do all along. He applied to enter the brand new Law School at UCLA.

A FEW MONTHS later, in June, I wore a cap and gown (the gown designated for an oversized male) which barely covered what seemed to be an unusually generous pregnancy. Three weeks after I graduated from UCLA, our son, Bobby, was born. To everyone's surprise, even the obstetrician's, he was eleven pounds, two ounces, and might have been cuter if he hadn't arrived with padded shoulders and what appeared to be nuts squirreled away in his cheeks. He was also the largest baby ever born in that hospital.

Everyone loved the idea but me. The nurses thought he was quite the handsome little fellow, and peppered me with quips. "We caught him sitting up, reading." "I expect he'll be walking to the car."

They never knew that I was mortified, that I imagined, in my young-girl ignorance, I must have eaten too much and created a monument to gluttony.

I couldn't wait to take him home.

Rob had no such thoughts. He was endlessly proud and took great pains filling out Bobby's baby book. When he came to a section labeled "Special Problems," he sat up straighter and wrote in his great, intimidating hand, "This baby *has* no problems!"

We'd had our son a whole week, now, and maternal pride had finally rushed over me like a tsunami on post-partum hormones. I, too, thought Bobby was perfect.

When I found Bobby's baby book years later, I read Rob's words with chagrin, shaking my head. Nobody who's ever been a parent for more than two weeks would taunt the humility gods with a statement like that!

Bobby started the ball rolling.

CHAPTER FIVE

The Moot Court Competition

I'VE NEVER WON an argument against Rob.

Which is not to say I've never gotten my own way, it just means I've never bested him verbally. If someone rated us on our oral confrontations, Rob would come off as a powerful William Jennings Bryant . . . whereas I, dogged and emotional and trying not to whine, would get a rating about equal to Marge Simpson. He uses words that cut like a scalpel. I fight back with timeworn clichés that are off the mark and slice no deeper than a hurled marshmallow.

I'm smarter now; I no longer do what I can't win at, and instead I take Rob on in ways that aren't so obvious.

But in 1953, when he was in his final year of law school, I hadn't yet seen him operate in any arena larger than our kitchen; I didn't know what he was capable of.

I soon found out.

DURING ROB'S THIRD year, a group of young California lawyers calling themselves the Junior Barristers, created a hypothetical legal case known as Roger Blackgold vs. U. R. Dutybound. This complex, at times humorous, petroleum conservation lawsuit was designed for the California law schools' moot court competition, meaning eight schools employed the same case.

As I recall the facts, Rob was defending U. R. Dutybound, maintaining staunchly that Blackgold had no right to be slurping oil sidewise by slant drilling under Dutybound's land. But let's be honest; the real issue, at first, was whether Rob and his UCLA partner, Daren Johnson, could out-argue two law students from Loyola.

The opposing teams met in Los Angeles—in a real courtroom before three real judges. Except for a bit of histrionics from Johnson (which even I knew was rarely seen in actual trials), and leaving out the Loyola man who referred to "my worthy opponents," in sneering overtones, the competition was breathtaking only to the wives.

To our huge delight, Rob and Daren won.

FOR THE NEXT month it was rumored around UCLA that their opponents from the University of Southern California Law School, were "out to get" UCLA in the second round. Somehow Johnson and Wills didn't take these rumors as seriously as their rivals hoped.

When the teams finally met in court, Johnson spoke first. Throughout his argument he kept raising his palms as though in supplication to heaven, and he also pointed, shrugged, and alternated between looks of pain and surprise, a performance worthy of a review in *Variety.*

Then came the first S.C. man, who strutted about like a legal peacock and decisively shredded every argument Johnson had made.

When it was Rob's turn, he ignored what everyone else had done and merely offered an uncluttered line of logic. With his arguments still ringing in my ears, the last S. C. man could have been accusing U. R. Dutybound of soliciting oilfield orgies and I wouldn't have noticed.

It seemed unreasonable, later, that a simple meal could transform two overbearing lawyers from U.S.C. into a couple of slim, eager boys who were actually likeable.

After dinner the judges spoke of "excellent arguments on both sides." And they gave the vote to UCLA!

Rob and I didn't drive home that night—we floated!

Far in the future, sometime after the bar exam, Wills and Johnson would argue the last round of the moot court competition against the winners from all the law schools in northern California. This time the argument would be held at The Bar Convention in Monterey—but it was a distant thing, and too much lay before them to think about it.

ON THE FIFTH of September, our third little boy, Eric, was born. After viewing him in the nursery, Rob came to my hospital room and said warmly, "We have a pretty good mold, babe, I wouldn't change a thing. He looks just like the others, but of course he's pretty small—only nine pounds, six ounces," which made me laugh. Our oldest, Bobby, had been eleven-two, and our second boy, Chris, only ten, and we seemed to be losing several ounces of baby with each go-around.

On October 1, three weeks after Eric's birth, Rob packed a suitcase to go take the bar exam. He had the dazed look of a man who is being led to the gas chamber and no longer cares. He seemed beyond discussing it.

"I'll be at the Mayflower Hotel, babe, if you need me," and he scooped up Bobby for a hug, patted Chris, and left us to go downtown for three days—just as someone turned up the thermostat in central Los Angeles.

On October second, the temperature in L. A. was ninety-seven, the next day, ninety-eight. In those days air-conditioning wasn't the norm, and the temperature in the Embassy Auditorium, where the bar exams were held, soared into the mid-nineties. Not only was the room filled with perspiring men (and a few women), but almost everyone had a portable typewriter of the old-fashioned, tap-tapping variety, so that the room was at once both redolent of nervous sweat and noisier than a 40's newsroom.

For three days I pictured Rob roasting and flunking.

I needn't have worried.

He came home the third night in a state of euphoria, and far from being exhausted he was buoyed by adrenaline and elated at the brilliance of the questions. When I asked about the heat he said, "Heat? That was the least of our worries. We were typing so fast we didn't even notice it!"

His mother, Ruth, who happened to be there, said, "Gracious, Rob!" and clacked her tongue sympathetically.

Rob described the bar exam, full of essay questions that literally crawled with issues, and his perception of the intense heat fading away each day, while the din of typewriters rose to a hellish clatter.

And then he abruptly changed the subject and brought up a topic that neither of us had really thought about in months. "Did I tell you that the moot court finals take place the day after tomorrow?"

"No!" cried Ruth, who now, in her older years, could turn tragic on a dime. "You're *not* going from one terrible ordeal to another!"

"Yep," said Rob, cheerfully. "That's exactly what I'm doing, Mother. It'll be hell, but I'm going."

Which is why we prepared to leave late the next afternoon to drive to Monterey, a distance of 350 miles . . . though Rob's mother rolled her eyes and seemed ready to weep. "Don't do it," she cried. "You're killing yourself, Rob! That's what you're doing—destroying yourself!"

Rob grinned and said he was still operating on excess adrenaline and could probably go on indefinitely.

Since Ruth's advice to her son during his first grueling year of law school had been, "Don't let them do this to you, Rob! You just show them—and quit!" neither of us was inclined to pay much heed to her admonishments.

Now Rob rolled down the window of our old green Nash, The Turtle, and waved goodbye. Ruth stood in the driveway with three-year-old Bobby on one side and eighteen-month-old Chris clinging to her skirt. "Don't overdo!" she called out one last time. "You hear?"

"I'll probably collapse from the strain," he yelled back, making a long face just to torture her. "See you in a couple of days—if I'm not dead."

Still, I wondered why we were going. That morning Rob had announced matter-of-factly, "You realize, Babe, this moot court thing is pretty much a lost cause. The respondents were winners in both the Northern and Southern law schools, and since we can't all argue the same side of the case, someone had to switch sides. Johnson and I lost the toss."

"Then why are we doing this, Rob?" I probably sounded like his mother.

He just looked at me and grinned. "Because I'm a masochist—why else?"

The news that day continued to spiral downward. Before noon, Darren Johnson called to tell us officiously that the rules had just been changed and there would now be a single winner from among the four contestants—winner take all. ("All" in this case being five hundred dollars worth of law books.) "I'm getting an early start," said Daren, laughing evilly. "Bringing along a trailer to haul back the books."

I looked at Rob. "You offered to kill him, right?"

"We'll just see what he puts in that trailer."

With tiny Eric in the backseat (he had to go because I was nursing), Rob and I started off cheerfully. Still high from the bar exam, he drove while I read him the facts on Roger Blackgold vs. U. R. Dutybound—though before we'd traveled ten miles he had begun abandoning his old friend, Dutybound, in a search for redeeming features in Blackgold. "This is amazing," he said. "There really are two sides to this case!"

Clouds scampered along overhead, and there was the feeling in our little car that we were merely pleasure jaunting up the coast—until abruptly Rob's adrenaline gave out.

Then the sun went down, and from the rear seat Eric started howling, so I had to bring him up front for supper.

Rob had not finished studying. Somehow he had to keep gathering facts about the wrong side of the case.

With Eric quiet again, I took over the driving and Rob felt around in the glove compartment for some kind of a light. "Nothing," he said. "Nothing anywhere. Wouldn't you know?"

When he spoke again his cheery mood had vanished. "No gambler would put money on this contest. When I got up this morning the odds of winning were two out of four. Now they're one out of four."

"I know," I said. "So why are we going?"

"As a matter of fact, I've been thinking about turning back."

"We could, you know."

I said it, but I knew he wouldn't. Not him. Turning back wasn't his style. This was the man who stuck with a madcap truck driver barreling down the Grapevine, and later, three bumbling contractors who wouldn't have done well building outhouses, and he never spoke of quitting. Instead he would grumble and swear and predict ultimate failure and make me wish *I'd* stayed home.

"One way or another," he said, "I've got to study." But the only interior light was a dim bulb *under* the glove compartment, that stayed lit only when the car door was open, as he discovered when he tentatively pushed his door open a crack. The light flickered on, but then the door slammed shut and out went the bulb.

Anyone else would have resigned himself to darkness. Instead, Rob rooted under the front seat and suddenly said, "Ah-ha!" and held up an old Arden milk bottle, replete with ancient smudges of dried milk. "By gum, it'll stay open now." He pushed against the door and wedged the glass bottle into the crack, and the ten-watt bulb under the glove compartment glowed faintly. With the wind hissing through the opening, Rob cork-screwed himself down under the glove compartment, grabbed his sheaf of papers, and slowly gathered a case for his once enemy, now devoted friend, Roger Blackgold.

In such a posture, he rode the rest of the way to Monterey.

It was ten-thirty at night when we arrived—so tired that we

paid scant attention when we ran into Daren Johnson at the hotel and he informed us, rather too cheerfully, that we'd missed dinner at the hotel and now all the restaurants were closed. He was still unbelievably upbeat—effervescing like Alka Seltzer. "Well, Rob, are you all ready for tomorrow?" he asked, and I swear he rubbed his hands together like Scrooge contemplating his next nickel.

His wife gave me a thin, sideways smile, indicating she wasn't ready at all.

Johnson started for the stairs. "See you down there bright and early, Rob. I'll have my trailer parked out front." He grinned wickedly and pulled his wife along. "Come on, Carmen." Laughing, they disappeared.

Rob studied until midnight, and then we turned out the light, planning to get up at seven.

About one A.M. Eric began to howl. And also at two and four, indicating a basic natal distrust common to Wills babies about being forced to sleep in strange places.

Dawn arrived at five-thirty and we might have slept right through it, except that somebody decided right then to attack the street under our window with a jackhammer. In disbelief we listened to the repetitive pounding of metal on cement. But Eric, who apparently found jackhammers soothing, slept like the baby he was. From under the pillows, where Rob and I had burrowed to escape the noise, it seemed unthinkable that in just a few hours he'd be addressing the entire California State Bar Convention.

It seemed unlikely he'd be able to speak at all.

Lying rigid as broom handles, we harbored separate grim thoughts of dumping water on the man in the street—except that would have meant getting out of bed. Rob said later he'd considered going home right after breakfast, and I thought he sounded serious, while I admitted to fantasies of pounding nails in the tires of Johnson's trailer.

With all hope of sleep finished, Rob and I lay in bed, stupefied, waiting for something else to happen—which, around seven, turned out to be the baby chiming in like a chorus with the jackhammer.

Rob wrenched himself to his feet. His face was ashen and his eyes rimmed with dark circles; he looked about fifty. "Oh boy," he muttered. "I'm sick. I'm nauseated."

One glance at his fierce expression made it clear there were no wifely words I could risk uttering.

Before I'd finished bathing Eric in the bathroom sink, Rob was telling me I'd better hurry and get downstairs to order breakfast or we wouldn't have any. I rushed out, leaving Rob shaving and the baby on the bed.

The waitress in the hotel dining room meandered between tables with a relaxed air. But she wasn't as slow as Rob, who apparently was never going to show up. I kept looking at my watch and looking at his bacon and eggs and looking toward the stairs, while the time got to be thirty, then twenty, then seventeen minutes to eight.

At fifteen minutes to the hour he showed up looking wretched. "The baby's been screaming the whole time you've been gone. I had to call a sitter. The manager sent someone up, and now Eric's quiet."

Oh, thank God. "You'd better eat," I said softly. "You need something."

"Eat? I can't *possibly* eat! I feel sick." He glanced at the fried eggs and said, "Ugh!"

Quickly he paid the bill and we were off—off to make Rob's grand debut before half the lawyers and judges in California, in the final and most impressive round of the moot court competition.

WHEN WE ARRIVED the crowd was all seated and the three other contestants and five judges were sitting on an open stage in front of the audience, though luckily they hadn't begun.

Rob joined the men on stage and I found a seat in the audience. Only a minute later the first participant stood up.

The other two men were from the University of San Francisco, having prevailed over Stanford, Cal Berkeley, Santa Clara, and Hastings. Somehow I expected them to look ferocious, or at least overbearing—they had, after all, been steady winners. To my surprise they just looked like boys. Daren Johnson seemed as formidable as any; his skills were obvious and he was no longer part of our team.

After awhile my mind wandered from the speeches, and I began thinking about our circumstances and how Rob had had no breakfast—and for that matter, no dinner the night before. And of course no sleep either. Obviously all those judges and lawyers would never know any of this, but physically he could not have been in worse shape.

When it was Rob's turn, I could hardly bear to watch. He began speaking in a voice of deadly calm, so deliberative that I was shocked. His words seemed to be coming through some kind of modulating screen, and frankly, I'd never heard him talk like that before.

The truth was, I thought he was going to faint, and I began sending him silent messages: Don't fall down, Rob. Don't keel over in front of all these people. Just finish. Stay on your feet. It'll be over in a minute. Keep standing—you can do it.

As I watched, I saw that he seemed unaware of his audience and of the other contestants, or even of himself. Calmly, very slowly, he directed his argument to the judges. To me it was the voice of a quiet, ponderous stranger—a hungry, over-worked, dog-tired, near-fainting stranger.

When he finally came to his conclusion, still speaking in that tone of lethal calm, I realized I hadn't actually heard a word of his argument. Only two things seemed important: he had finished. And he was still standing.

Now that he hadn't disgraced himself, we could go home happy. I couldn't wait to go fetch the baby and get out of there.

After the last speaker returned to his seat, and we'd all stood while the five judges left the stage, I wiped clammy hands across my gabardine skirt and turned to the lady next to me, because I simply had to speak to someone. "Oh God, I'm glad that's over!"

She smiled sympathetically.

The audience chatted in subdued voices for a few minutes and presently the judges returned. I was paying them only half attention until one of them stepped to the front of the stage and in a matter-of-fact voice made an incredible announcement: "The winner for the best oral argument is Robert Wills!"

I gasped. He'd won it all. An astonished squeal took me by surprise and I clapped my hand over my mouth. It wasn't possible!

I whispered to myself, "I don't believe it!" And then I turned to the lady next to me and said, "I don't believe it!" and she smiled again, but still I kept saying those words over and over in my head. It simply couldn't have happened. Not to Rob. Not today.

People around me were smiling and clapping.

I stared at him up there on the stage, looking so pleased, shaking hands with all the judges, courteous and gracious and almost matter-of-fact, as though it were someone else's victory.

Rob was now the moot court champion for the State of California. And no one could take that away.

Presently he came down from the stage and when we left the hall it was as though we were propelled by feet not our own. Voices not our own said "Thank you," and "Yes, we're very happy," and "I'm glad you liked it." We couldn't have known that this triumph would exceed even the joy of passing the bar.

Later we were invited to the assembly luncheon as guests of the convention, where we took our baby, and once again ate almost nothing, as people were exclaiming over the infant and over Rob's performance, and we were smiling, smiling with pleasure. It's hard to stuff food into the middle of a smile.

By now food no longer seemed necessary.

And then we were heading home again in The Turtle, its sagging rear made worse with some forty volumes of *West's California Digest* and other legal tomes. Never, not once, had we pictured ourselves returning this way.

"Well, Rob," I said, "you outmaneuvered them all—the baby, the jackhammers and Daren Johnson's trailer."

"Yeah," he said, laughing. "Pretty nice, huh babe?"

Very nice, I thought, *except for one thing: there goes my last hope of ever winning an argument from you!*

Rob was one of the early graduates of UCLA law school.

Three boys should have been enough family for anybody.

Bobby, Chris, and Eric, circa 1954.

The obstetrician apologized for a fourth boy . . .

After 4 boys, a girl looked mighty good.

Sometimes the mob could be fun, even without Bobby.

Lemonade? In the rain?

CHAPTER SIX

The Underground Fort

TEN YEARS LATER we'd become the parents of six children—five boys and a girl—and it was assumed by those who knew us only in passing that we were devoted Catholics, when in fact we were simply passionate Presbyterians.

Once in a while I thought back to those childhood dreams Rob and I had entertained as youngsters, those wholly unrealistic images of ourselves as adults. For a short while Rob imagined he'd be a railroad engineer, and later, with a dawning love of the outdoors, a forest ranger.

I entertained no such lofty ideals. I saw myself as a bride. As though being a bride was a permanent state of affairs, as though brideship was a condition that lasted through maturity and on into senility. How else can one explain a vision that never carried me beyond a few golden moments of twirling before a mirror in a silken wedding gown, radiant to the point of luminescence, and on to a dizzying, forever-float down a church aisle with everyone looking and gasping? Oh, what a fairy vision of a bride I'd conjured up, what a back-lit center of attention I imagined I'd be!

That walk was obviously meant to last forever. Certainly no competing image ever arose to explain what I might be doing after the bride bit.

It was all so ironic.

By 1962, surrounded by half a dozen children in all stages from pupa to butterfly, I was thinking back on how the dream had gone astray: after all my girlish fantasies about a wedding as opulent as a coronation, I'd settled for Spartan vows and no real wedding at all. And having given no thought whatever to children, I was now the mother of six—and I swear they snuck up on me, one by one, when I wasn't looking.

Along with everything else, the humor in our lives had taken a twist. The funny things that once happened to us when it was just Rob and me squaring off against the world, had now become the craziness created by the two of us pitted against a defiant army we'd created ourselves from scratch—a phalanx of children that surrounded us on all sides.

We'd moved, of course. No army could possibly be garroted in such tiny quarters as that first house in the San Fernando Valley. Together, Rob and I chose to locate miles away in cooler Orange County, though I maintain he deliberately cultivated a twenty-eight-mile commute to his legal work in Long Beach, a distance which struck him as a bare-minimum separation from the confusion he left each morning. Sometimes he said, only half in jest, "This place is like a circus without the elephants."

In North Tustin, California, we built a modest house on a half-acre of land that backed up to an orange grove. Our children loved the new location; they had endless space for their endless projects, and even better, they could roam unfettered through the grove and stage little wars and bomb each other with oranges.

By 1962 our oldest, Bobby, was eleven and a half, and our youngest, Kirk, only two, and we'd learned what every parent of more than one discovers sooner or later—no matter how painstakingly you work at molding your kids, they will turn out different than you planned, and in fact no two will be remotely alike, and if you don't believe that's possible in a nice, consistent, even-tempered environment, just study a few snowflakes.

WE'D KNOWN FROM the start that Bobby was the stubborn one. Long-faced and quietly intense, he was a skinny child who said frequently, "I don't *want* to do what everyone else has done. I want to be *different.*" From his earliest years he was propelled by an inner force that drove him—not to play like other children, God forbid—but to re-make, improve, or otherwise conquer his childhood toys. He didn't *play* with his train set. He built a virtual train-switching yard that crept across the cement and devoured our patio.

Sometimes as he worked, he wheezed. But obstinate beyond reason, he said, "It's not asthma. I'm not sick." I was always arguing with him. "Bobby, stop fixing your train set and come to dinner." He came when he felt like it.

Bobby wasn't the one getting raised, I was. In his own dogged way, he trained me to equal him in stubbornness. The problem was, I kept imagining myself as the boss who ought to be making the decisions . . . whereas he saw himself as a youthful Alexander the Great who couldn't be conquered. We lived our lives in a clash of images.

Soon Rob and I discovered he had dreams, but what we didn't know at first was their width and breadth . . . that an eleven-year-old could think of himself in global terms, that he could vow privately to create a competition-size environment deep in the ground. And then actually do it.

Bobby confided his plans one morning at breakfast. "Dad, I'm going to dig the world's biggest underground fort." He said it just like that. No buildup. No explanation. No preparatory speeches.

Rob looked up from his puffed wheat. "How will you know it's the world's biggest, Bobby?" Rob was trying to be serious, but of course he wasn't, how could he be? Bobby was just a child, and even to me this was idle conversation.

Bobby's long face changed subtly, took on greater eagerness, more resolve. His voice conveyed his certainty. "I'll just know, Dad. I will." And I swear, we almost believed him.

And so began "The Year of the Underground Fort."

BOBBY DIDN'T WASTE any time. Unlike other eleven-year-olds who begin a project after breakfast and abandon it by supper, Bobby recruited his brothers with an intensity that would have made the Marines proud. He did, indeed, intend to dig for himself and his siblings a noteworthy underground fort, and to that end he conscripted his next-oldest brother, Chris, and then our third son, Eric. By noon, the three of them were hard at work.

I heard them through the kitchen window. The far side of the yard became a noisy, industrial place. They worked for hours.

But two shoveling brothers didn't live up to Bobby's expectations. "You've got to dig faster!" he cried, inciting them to greater effort. Willing to tunnel at a fiendish pace himself, he was dismayed to find that his brothers worked at something less than the speed of a steam shovel.

Clearly, help was needed. As only Bobby could do, he brought in friends, expanding his sphere of influence outward block by block, like a creeping flood, until every neighborhood child with access to a shovel had convened in our backyard. I watched and was mostly amused.

For days, then weeks, our yard was never quiet. The clanking of shovels and the shrill sounds of youthful voices dominated our half acre until our backyard was like an over-subscribed union job, with half the workers bent to the task and the other half leaning on their shovels.

Day after day Bobby led the charge, shoveling furiously one minute, exhorting his youthful minions the next.

Meanwhile, the mounds of dirt grew, and so, presumably, did the underground fort. I never saw it up close until the project was nearly at an end (when Chris, cheerfully but insistently, led me down into the bowels of the earth), but I did see that Bobby had hardened into steel; I could feel his willpower all the way to the kitchen. It hardly seemed possible that such a young boy could keep such tight control over what was basically an unmanageable company of slackers.

And then two things happened. Bobby's friends, and soon even his brothers, grew weary of being the indentured servants of a relentless taskmaster. "I can't dig anymore," said Chris one day, walking toward the house. "I'm tired."

I happened to be watching through the kitchen window and wondered how Bobby would handle the loss of his best worker—Chris the faithful, Chris the determined shoveler.

For seconds Bobby stared in horror, and then he ran after his brother. "You *can't be tired!*" he howled. "You're not tired, Chris, you know you're not. You want this fort a lot, you want it as much as I do."

Chris gave him a glance and kept walking.

Giving up on mind control, Bobby did a quick, dancing side-step, trying to cut off his brother's escape.

Chris wouldn't be stopped. He just moved deftly around his older brother and continued toward the house.

Bobby followed, desperation on his long face. "Please, Chris, come back. I need you. I can't do it without you. Everyone needs you. Please."

At last Chris paused and simply looked at him.

With a glint in his eyes, Bobby pulled out his trump card. Like a gambler, he slapped it on the table. "Chris, if you keep digging, I'll . . . I'll give you my marbles. All of them. Even the aggies." Anxiously he waited to see if Chris would succumb to this, the ultimate bribe.

"The aggies?" Chris stopped to consider, letting the silence grow, thinking hard about Bobby's offer. Finally he raised his eyes and said with his own fierce determination, "All right, Bobby. I'll do it. But don't yell at me anymore, okay? I don't like being yelled at."

"You'll dig?" said Bobby.

"For awhile." With slow steps Chris turned back toward the fort. Halfway across the yard he called out, "You don't have to give me your aggies, Bobby."

The second happening was bigger, much harder to solve. Bobby's asthma, which he'd had since early childhood, flared up and became so severe that at night we could hear the sounds of his wheezing in the hall outside his room. Still he said stubbornly, "The fort's not hurting me. Don't you think I'd know if it was?"

Rob and I finally recognized the truth—that the spores, molds, and fungus inherent in all soil were making him worse. The fort had to go.

But it took both of us and the advice from a doctor and our combined willpowers to bring Bobby to a halt. And even then we might not have succeeded, had Rob not taken an extraordinary step: one night, by the light of the moon, he went outside with a shovel and for hours he relentlessly restored the earth to Bobby's underground fort.

BOBBY GAVE UP with resignation, even grace. And that was only the beginning of his trauma.

Because his asthma was now so severe, Rob and I were forced to consider our last resort—a home for asthmatic children, an institution in Denver where the minimum stay was two years.

Telling Bobby he had to leave all of us, his brothers, his parents, his grandparents, for two years was one of the hardest things we ever did. And harder still when he didn't argue. As he would do in later years, Bobby fought back when a fight was possible, and when it wasn't, he just coped.

Bobby's underground fort attracted all the neighborhood kids.

CHAPTER SEVEN

The Great Sequoia Hike

NONE OF US wanted it, but Bobby would be leaving soon.

With our son's departure imminent, Rob and I scrambled to soften the pain that we knew was coming. Maybe if he had a last, great weekend, we thought . . . which is how we happened to take the four oldest boys to the High Sierras, a kind of final-hurrah for a departing son.

Determined to hike efficiently, Rob had studied catalogues and ordered the latest marvels in deep-woods engineering—two Mountain Master back-packs touted as offering perfect weight-distribution over the hiker's body. "These may be expensive," he said, holding up one of the khaki green contraptions and fingering the aluminum frame, "but if they're half as good as the Mountain Master people claim, they'll be worth it."

"Money's not important when it comes to our backs," I echoed. Then somehow I got the message confused. In an odd twist of logic, perfect weight distribution began to mean the extra weight disappears. Suddenly additional ounces meant nothing.

Feeling smug at being so wonderfully organized, I filled our packs with everything we could possibly need: canned pork-and-beans, frozen meat, canned soups, dried eggs, pancake mix, jars of coffee, sugar, and syrup, extra jackets, a flashlight, and various toilet articles and drugs. This in addition to raisins and candy bars, sacks of nuts, cooking pots and a frying pan. At the time it all seemed quite reasonable. We would, after all, be out of touch with civilization for most of two days.

At the start of a rustic trail in Sequoia National Park, Rob and I squirmed into our Mountain Masters and helped Bobby and Chris with their bundles—all the sleeping bags rolled into two fat sausages. Chris was now eleven-and-a-half and almost as tall as Bobby, who was nearly thirteen. Eric, ten, and Kenny, seven, carried tiny knapsacks on their tiny shoulders.

Rob had someone snap our picture, which shows the six of us strapped into our loads, smiling, fresh, and eager. "Wouldn't it be nice," Rob said, "if all our trips got off to this kind of easy start?"

Our destination was Bearpaw Meadow, eleven miles along the High Sierra Trail. As I looked toward the forest, the air seemed to shimmer with its very cleanness, and sunlight produced shadows as sharp as etchings. The woods smelled good, like damp leaves and sap. In the sun it was warm, in the deeper forest briskly cool.

"Let's go," I said, eager to test our equipment. So Rob led off, his plump Mountain Master giving him the proportions of a hump-backed grizzly. Strung out on the trail behind him, the boys and I trudged along at just the right intervals to breathe each other's dust.

As we started up the first small incline, I could tell that our backpacks were indeed well-designed, for I could feel the weight in several unexpected places—not just in my shoulders, but also in my arms, calves, and lower spine.

Then the trail grew steeper, and I began to wonder if I hadn't overdone the packing a tiny bit . . . Did we really *need* four tins of pork-and-beans?

We'd been walking silently for maybe twenty minutes when I thought I heard a groan up ahead. "You okay, Rob?" I called out.

He didn't answer, nor did he slow the pace. But minutes later he stopped and sagged against a tree.

Catching up, I saw rivulets of sweat making their way down the sides of his face, and he was bent low, massaging his legs. "Son-of-a-bitch!" he said. "My knees!"

Momentarily overtaken by the guilt which I keep handy for such occasions, I started to apologize. Then stopped. He *knew* what I'd been packing and he hadn't said anything . . . and anyway, I was carrying my share.

But not very well. I found my own tree to lean against and felt a dull ache recede from my muscles. It appeared the Mountain Master people had kept their promise; whatever sensations you got, you got them everywhere.

For several minutes Rob and I rested in disgruntled silence, dismayed that we were so much weaker than we'd imagined. Neither of us felt like talking.

The boys, on the other hand, seemed annoyingly fresh. Bobby's thin face was alert, brighter than normal, and Chris beamed at us out of chipmunk cheeks, his usual good-natured self. The two carried their packs as casually as pocket handkerchiefs.

"This is neat," said Eric, "isn't it neat, Kenny?" and Kenny nodded, and with much squealing the two dashed off after a ground squirrel.

After awhile we set off again.

But the respite hadn't helped. If anything, my load was heavier, in fact inexplicably weighty, as though something big had crawled inside.

I wasn't watching Rob anymore or the redwoods or the carpet of ferns. I was watching the ground, staring at dust, staring at the trail. The minutes passed, and it no longer mattered how the weight was distributed. The whole blasted load could have hung from my neck, for all the help I was getting from that perfect engineering. I felt like I was hauling a Steinway.

Bearpaw Meadow was no longer attainable. Eleven miles or one mile, what was the difference, I was never going to get there.

Suddenly I couldn't walk another step. With a last surge of will I gasped my way to a big rock and sagged out from under the crushing load.

Rob stopped too, and in one swift motion he jerked the pack off his body and dropped it on the ground. "My knees are through," he declared. "Finished."

In our separate foul moods, we stood there panting. The boys watched in surprise as Rob roused enough to drag his Mountain Master off the trail, growling that he didn't care whether he ever saw the damned thing again. "For two cents I'd leave it right here."

"What if somebody steals it?" Eric asked. He was cute and blue-eyed, just outgrowing his baby softness.

Rob laughed without mirth. "I'd like to see the thief who's strong enough to haul it away!"

So this was it, I thought, Rob and I finally felled by our possessions, with too much to carry in either direction.

Six of us milled on the trail while we tried to decide what to do. After several irresolute minutes, Bobby offered casually, "I'll carry your pack, Dad."

Rob and I stared at him and shook our heads in unison. "You can't," Rob said. "If I can't, you can't."

"Sure I can," said Bobby, and he hoisted Rob's pack onto his scrawny shoulders. "See?"

Rob smiled. "Bobby, you haven't tried walking yet."

"I can walk," Bobby said, and started off.

With that Chris picked up my pack. "You take my stuff, Mom. It's light."

He was right, it was. So I carried Chris's load and Rob took Bobby's, and the six of us moved off down the trail again with our oldest boys in front, where anyone that strong deserved to be.

From time to time Rob and I exchanged incredulous glances, amazed at this turning point, that our roles had been reversed with two pre-teens. But the bigger boys never said a word. Not a complaint, not a murmur.

They carried those Mountain Masters all the way to Bearpaw Meadow, they slept on the ground that night, and Sunday morning they hauled their loads five miles up and down a precipitous, winding trail to Hamilton Lake and out again, then back the eleven miles to our parked car. Thirty-two miles in thirty-six hours.

The only time they complained was at Sunday morning's breakfast. They didn't like the scrambled eggs, which I'd made from a dried packet and a cup of stream water and which cooked up into a dark, gray-green viscous blob, a mess that only Dr. Seuss could love. "I've never seen green eggs!" Bobby said, screwing up his long face.

"I'm sorry, Mom, it looks like a big, squashed slug," said Chris.

"Pancakes, then?" I asked, tossing the green eggs into the campfire because nobody else wanted them either.

Kenny watched the eggs as they sizzled. "Good you burned 'em, Mom. They coulda made some bear sick."

But the pancakes, too, turned a strange color in addition to being dense and hard. I was finally glad we'd hauled in the heavy, canned baked beans.

Sunday night we ran out of everything except food (of which we had enough to take us through the winter), out of time, daylight, and energy. We'd tried to go too far, lingered to catch a few fish too many. But we had to get back to Orange County that night because our flight to Denver left the next morning.

As the light faded and the miles didn't, Rob said, "Boys, we've got to keep going," and Bobby nodded and led us down the murky trail as though he always went hiking in inky darkness. He still hadn't mentioned the piano on his shoulders, nor had Chris.

Behind Bobby came Rob with a wavering flashlight, then Chris and Eric, both resolutely quiet, and finally Kenny, who began asking, "What if we see a bear?"

From the rear I told him we probably wouldn't see any bears, we were making too much noise, and Kenny said in a nervous, pipey voice, "How do you know? Are you sure?"

"Yes," I said, and yearned to have this over with, not because of the bears or the darkness but because I felt like I'd already walked a thousand miles.

About ten-thirty Rob's flashlight gave out and we all disappeared.

Such an irony, I thought. *All those canned goods and only one flashlight.* An eerie tension crept over us, not helped when little Kenny, thin and skittish as a bird, began to whimper. "I'm scared. There *might* be a bear."

"There's no bear, Kenny," I promised.

"I think I hear a mountain lion."

"It's just Bobby stepping on a twig."

"What if a cougar jumps out?"

"Cougars won't bother us," I said. "They're afraid of people."

"But you don't know, Mom. You don't know."

With increasing anguish he named all the wild predators one by one, the spiders, the snakes, the wolves, while up front somewhere Bobby searched out the trail.

For the next two hours Kenny clung to my hand and sobbed into the night.

Periodically Bobby called out the distances. "Mile five," he sang out, because he'd somehow managed to spot the wooden marker nailed to a tree. And later, "Mile four." When he missed mile three, the tension became so thick even Rob sounded edgy.

By then Kenny was crying hard enough for all of us.

SOMETIME AFTER MIDNIGHT we emerged from the forest and staggered up to our station wagon.

As Rob lifted the pack from Bobby's narrow shoulders, he clapped his hand on Bobby's arm. "You guys were terrific."

Bobby smiled and nodded a private, satisfied smile. The moment was vintage Bobby, the start of the quiet triumphs we would one day see so vividly. I thought it odd that he didn't seem weary at all.

The boys all climbed into the back of our large station wagon and immediately fell asleep.

Rob said he'd take us down the mountain and I could drive the rest of the way home.

Back on level roads once more, we stopped to switch drivers. When I stepped out of the car on my side, a surprise was waiting.

With no warning whatsoever—before I'd taken a single step—my legs gave way and I sank to the ground like a collapsing card table.

I sat there, startled; my legs had never behaved like that before.

From the pavement, wanting to tell him what had happened, I looked through the open car door toward Rob. I expected to see him standing there, waiting. But he wasn't. He was sitting in a heap on the ground. Like me, he'd stepped out and buckled and gone down.

As I drove the rest of the way home to Orange County, I wondered if there wasn't a better plan than taking Bobby to Denver. For a whole weekend he hadn't wheezed once. No coughing, no fighting for breath.

Perhaps instead of the Home for Asthmatic Children, we ought to send him off to the High Sierras with a thirty-pound pack on his back.

We didn't look like this after covering 32 miles in 36 hours.

CHAPTER EIGHT

The Neuschwanstein Castle

BOBBY KNEW HOW to get to us. I swear, kids are born with parent-torturing genes. Just back from his two years at the Home for Asthmatic Children, Bobby was spiritless and resentful. He wouldn't look at us, wouldn't answer questions except in monosyllables, wouldn't smile. At home he walked around with his head hanging down. He wanted us to feel rotten.

Well, sure enough we did. And never mind that his asthma was now nearly gone.

Rob and I flailed about, deciding at last to surround him with wonderful trips—rather like trying to wall off a disease. We'd taken him to the mountains before he left, and now we were offering Bobby and Chris a trip to Europe.

"Getting away should do wonders for him," said Rob, "make Bobby forget those miserable two years."

"If anything can," I said.

"Babe, everyone feels better after a trip."

Whether our two boys really liked the second trip, we were never sure. But it was certainly instructive for us.

In our naiveté, Rob and I had imagined that Bobby, 15, and Chris, 13, would be endlessly intrigued by strange countries and different customs. Maybe even dazzled.

Uh . . . not quite.

IT WAS ROB who inadvertently found a way to capture Bobby's attention. We had just landed at Heathrow, where porters flocked to gather the luggage of incoming travelers. "We aren't rich," Rob announced firmly, waving off the red caps, "and nobody in our group is infirm. Hiring porters is a luxury. We will carry our own suitcases." (Airport luggage carts and wheeled suitcases were still unknown.)

But Rob reckoned without the solution-minded spirit of Bobby, who was still so spindly after his two years away that we wondered what, if anything, he'd been willing to eat. Not much, it appeared.

In any case, as we were running for our first train—four of us lugging big suitcases, panting and huffing and lumbering alongside the tracks—Bobby happened to spot a huge, four-wheeled wooden cart sitting next to a post. At the moment unattended, the cart clearly called out to him, because he pulled up short with a surprised grin. "Here, Mom!" Bobby cried with newfound spirit, "put your bag on this," and he loaded up my suitcase (which I gave him joyfully), and then all the others, and grabbing the metal handle, he easily ran the length of the train. *Well, Bobby,* I thought, *isn't this nice! What a clever son!*

Never mind the curious stares he attracted from surprised porters along the way. An inventive lad who regularly rode strange contraptions through our neighborhood, Bobby was accustomed to stares and extravagant double-takes. Besides, nobody was stopping him, were they?

Well, they didn't stop him in Britain, where porters, like everyone else, consider politeness a virtue.

But now Bobby was into this, he considered it a game, and he began running off with porter's carts in countries where they are not so polite, and before long I was able to translate the word "no" in every country where the trains ran.

Sometimes Bobby assigned the job to Chris. "Move it, Chris!" Bobby shouted, and he hopped aboard and let Chris propel him and the luggage across the station as though they were competitors in a bed-pushing contest. Suddenly their luggage romps were looking less like the deeds of Boy Scouts and more like embarrassing pranks.

A few porters were so amazed at the boys' audacity that they stopped giving chase and merely stood shaking their heads. Others ran ahead and tried to head them off mid-station.

A few—usually the Germans, who are less flexible—seized the cart and emptied it on the spot. Bobby merely stood by and smiled. "It's okay, Mom," he said, a sign that he was relinquishing that cart, but no guarantee he wouldn't run off and find another.

Somehow he never noticed that he'd lost me, that not all of us still loved his efforts. Naturally averse to hostile humans of all nationalities, I was now often mortified, wanting nothing more than to distance myself from my outrageous son. "Go away, Bobby," I hissed, pretending I didn't know him, "I'll carry my own bags, okay?" and I tried to move away from him—away from his big grin and his mountain of suitcases and his entourage of shouting porters.

Eventually I saw by the look in Bobby's eyes that the cart capers had become more than transportation for luggage—they were a test of wits. Every cart successfully abducted, every porter confounded, was racked up somewhere in his brain as a point in the win column. He had concocted for himself a kind of movable chess game where success was tallied according to who retained final possession of the wheeled conveyance. With Chris providing diversionary moves, Bobby had turned the train station frolics into a highlight of his trip. And he was laughing.

But wait . . . wasn't that why we'd come?

IT WAS AT the Zurich train station that our family left its most indelible impression. There, the porter contest had become particularly contentious. The Zurich red caps *really* didn't want Bobby and Chris using their carts, and the boys had left hollering, crimson-faced porters in all parts of the train station.

As we headed for the 9:01 train with eight minutes to spare, it appeared the conflict would soon end. But we were no sooner aboard the train than Rob and I realized that neither of us could remember the name of the little lakeside town we'd picked out on a map. With first class passes that let us hop on anywhere, we had no tickets to clue us in.

The two of us decided we'd better figure out in a hurry where we were going, and a friendly conductor standing in the train vestibule offered to help. After we'd tried in vain to describe our destination and he'd rattled off a number of unfamiliar-sounding towns, we grew desperate and asked, "This *is* the 9:01?"

He said no, it was the 9:05!

With that, everyone panicked. The boys quickly jumped off, taking half the suitcases, and Bobby (of course), ran off for a cart. As a last resort before we fled for the 9:01, Rob had the conductor write down a few names, and there, at last, was our town. "Zug!" we cried. "That's it! This *is* the right train!"

At that moment the train started to move.

And now Rob and I were in the vestibule, slowly picking up speed, and the boys were on the platform with half the luggage.

What followed was bedlam, as those of us still on the train prepared to get off, and those who were off tried to get on. I took one look at my children standing alone on the platform and, seizing two of the nearest cases, I hopped off.

But Chris and Bobby, guessing this was our train, began running down the platform hurling suitcases up to Rob.

It suddenly appeared that I must get back on.

Chris, dealing with two fairly light bags, had put them both aboard, but Bobby, whose big blue bag was full of lead, or its equivalent, could hardly get his piece off the ground.

An empty baggage car went by, and I was about to throw my two suitcases in and myself afterwards, when I saw Bobby lifting and grunting, trying to get his heavy bag airborne. At the same moment I realized my skirt was so tight that only the greatest of gymnastic feats would put me aboard.

Meanwhile, the train was picking up speed and carrying with it our leader, the money, and everything else that mattered.

By now, Chris and Bobby and I, huffing and frantic, had stopped running.

At last certain he was more or less on his own runaway steed and would never be joined by his family, Rob did what he had to do. He threw a few pieces overboard. Then, with his arms full of luggage, he jumped.

Behind him, the conductor stood in the vestibule watching in horror. I saw him shaking his head, saw him mouth the words, "Oh! Oh! Oh!"

The train moved faster.

Even as Rob made the leap, I was distracted by a great clattering and banging behind me, and I turned to see Bobby's latest luggage cart rolling into the channel once occupied by the train. The enormous wooden thing got hung up, mid-plunge, and the last I saw of it, it was partly down in the pit, tilted crazily, with several irate porters lunging after it. I thought, *I'm glad I'll never see you fellows again.*

I turned back to Rob. To my horror, he was lying on the cement with arms and legs in the air, like an overturned turtle. His jump had looked safe enough, and it was hard to imagine how he'd gotten upended, but there he was, and of course we all rushed over to help. He got up slowly, so physically undone he could hardly speak.

"Are you hurt?" Chris asked, and Rob muttered, "Of course I'm hurt!"

Bobby began darting about, gathering luggage. "The cars were moving, Dad. You should have hit the ground running."

"I should have stayed on the goddamned train!"

Doing a Jackie Gleason slow burn, Rob brushed off his pants and arms, then began inspecting himself . . . and discovered that he was indeed hurt and the pain was coming from his left thigh. He looked down. A toothpick was poking through his gray slacks and straight into his leg.

"Good God!" he said, and slowly extracted the pick. In thick silence, three of us toted the luggage and, with Rob hobbling stiffly, we retreated into the station to wait for the next train to Zug.

Later, when he could smile again, Rob said, "I know where the toothpick came from—it was in my pants pocket." He watched a knot of travelers moving purposefully through the station. "I always thought the Swiss were cool and distant. After today, I can imagine what they think of us."

"So can I," said Bobby. "They think we're schizo. On the train, off the train, on the train. Like crazy people. I bet they'll be glad when we're gone."

IT WAS LATE in the day when the four of us arrived at the glistening white fairy-tale Neuschwanstein castle in Bavaria, a relatively new castle nestled picturesquely in a lush forest. Out of time, but intent on viewing this pristine landmark anyway, we'd decided that an hour of castle peeping was better than nothing.

As we approached, however, the ticket taker was already making noises about closing (much earlier than the literature said) and how we had so little time left we wouldn't get to see anything. "We're here," Rob mumbled to me, "and we'll never get back," and to her he said, "If it's all right with you, we'll just look around quickly and leave."

The woman shrugged. She'd no doubt seen her share of witless tourists who imagined they could do seven countries in six days and therefore a whole castle in twenty minutes.

I remember climbing a narrow stone staircase, swimming upstream against a flood of departing visitors . . . then on an upper floor, darting in and out of sitting rooms and bedrooms, catching glimpses of dark woods and tapestry bedspreads and paintings of nude, bosomy women hanging on the walls, and giving none more than a cursory glance. *This may be a modern castle, but modern is a relative term.*

I also remember thinking, suddenly, that maybe it was getting a bit late, because the castle had grown eerily silent.

The four of us met in an upstairs hallway. Chris said with a grin, "Did you see the pictures, Bobby?" and Bobby said, "What pictures?"

"You know—in the bedrooms."

"Oh . . . you mean the paintings. Sure, I saw 'em." He shrugged. "The women were all fat."

"They were naked."

"Yeah. Naked and fat." He looked up and down the hall. "I don't think anybody's left around here."

"No way," said Chris. "They would have sent somebody up here to get us."

Rob laughed. "They wouldn't leave a bunch of strangers alone in the castle."

"You know they wouldn't," I said.

"Then how come it's so quiet?" said Bobby, and Chris said, "Maybe we should leave now."

With growing apprehension, the four of us hurried down the echoing stairs to the entryway. And sure enough, the heavy, carved castle door was closed and the ticket taker gone.

"They probably left the door unlocked," said Bobby, and tried the handle. He was wrong. The door was definitely locked.

We stood in the richly tiled, oak-beamed entry hall looking around in dismay. All this elegance, and we wanted no part of it. I tried to find words to make us feel lighter, less like prisoners. "The bedrooms were kind of nice," I said, and the other three said nice or not, they didn't want to sleep in them. They threw me looks—the wicked stepmother offering them poisoned apples. The distinction between *visiting* a castle and being *locked up* in a castle struck home with great clarity.

"We have to do something pretty quick," said Rob. "It's getting dark."

"They must have electricity," I offered, at which Rob exploded. "I really don't give a damn whether they have electricity or not. I'm not spending the night in some glitzy Bavarian castle," and with that he began trying nearby windows.

All of them were locked. Chris and Bobby tried other windows. Also locked.

We stopped and looked at each other. We were beginning to feel desperate.

There was only one more window in our immediate vicinity, and Rob walked over without much hope and gripped the frame and gave it a mighty upward push. To our relief, the ancient wooden pieces creaked apart with the scrape of wood on wood, then slowly separated, leaving a small open space.

"Wow!" cried Bobby. "You did it, Dad. We're outta here!"

Rob poked his head through the opening and looked down. "Maybe we are and maybe we aren't," he said slowly. "This window is not exactly at ground level."

Chris went to look. "Geez! That's a seven foot jump!" He turned back to me. "You think you can jump seven feet, Mom?"

"She can do it," declared Bobby. "I know she can make it. You can do the jump, can't you, Mom?"

Why was he always so positive about things like this? What made him ascribe to others the qualities native only to himself? I took my turn looking out the window, and indeed, the distance did seem formidable. But down there among the lawns and hedges was freedom, and up here, seven feet above ground was prison. A tapestry-filled, elegantly furnished, lovingly-cared-for prison. But a prison, nevertheless. "I don't know," I said. "What makes you guys think I can leap out a window wearing a skirt?"

"Hike it up," said Bobby. "That'll free up your legs. You have to relax, Mom. You're a better jumper than you think."

Oh right Bobby. I wanted to laugh. *All that jumping you see me do around home.*

Bobby, of course, went first. Athlete that he was, he edged through the window, sailed past the hedges, and landed prettily on the grass. Chris went next, made a clean lawn landing, and called back to Rob, "You need us to catch you, Dad?"

"I think I can handle it," said Rob, and pulled himself onto the windowsill and jumped, but not quite far enough. He landed in a deep hedge and had to claw his way out.

"Try for the hedge, Babe," he called up to me. "It's actually not too bad."

Of course it's bad, I thought, looking down. *Leaping into shrubbery is always bad.* But I couldn't stay there alone. Hoisting my skirt, I pulled myself to the sill. If Bobby was so confident of my jumping skills, I supposed there was nothing for it but to jump. And out I went.

As I landed in the hedge, my skirt flew up over my head and blinded me, and there I was, barelegged, unable to see, and buried in shrubbery. Not exactly the expected end to a castle viewing. I flailed about, trying to escape.

"You see, Mom?" Bobby crowed as he extracted me from the deep, deep hedge. "I knew you could jump!"

"No you didn't, Bobby. You only knew you could talk me into it!"

The boys, of course, thought the castle tour was perfect, maybe the best part of the trip, and to our surprise, for days we entertained ourselves and others with stories about our "great escape."

Even today, when the conversation turns to foreign adventures, we're apt to say, "Did we ever tell you about the time we had to leap out a window in the Neuschwanstein castle?"

I RECALL VERY little about the Amsterdam Hilton Hotel, beyond the fact that it was surprisingly modern, that Holland seemed a very long way from home, and the setting was perhaps a bit elegant for a family with two teenage boys.

Wanting some peace, Rob and I gave the boys their own room, and the two of us started to unpack. It was late afternoon and we'd just begun to change when we heard an odd noise, a kind of big electrical pop, and all the lights went out. We were on the seventh floor, and we threw on clothes and dashed into the hall. And so did everyone else. All up and down the hall, doors opened, and surprised people poured into the nearly black corridors.

In the midst of all the cries and fumbling in the dark, Bobby and Chris appeared. Chris dragged us back into our room and turned to Bobby. "Tell them," he said.

"Tell us what?" said Rob.

"Tell them what you did."

"Which was?" Rob waited.

"I twirled the lamp," said Bobby.

"I don't understand."

"It was a table lamp," said Chris.

"I twirled it," Bobby explained without enthusiasm. "You know. I swung the lamp around by the cord."

"Why?" said Rob.

Exactly, I thought. *Why would a boy want to swing a table lamp like a lasso? Why?*

A shrug. "Just to see it spin, I guess. And suddenly there was this giant spark. And then a big pop." An unintended grin escaped his lips. "And then all the lights went out."

"That was you?" cried Rob. "That was you who pitched the whole seventh floor into darkness? Good God."

We didn't know what to do next, whether to lie low or try to sneak out. Certainly Rob was not charmed by the thought of paying to restore all that electricity. How much does it cost, anyway, to bring back the lights for an entire hotel floor?

"Maybe we could just go somewhere for dinner," offered Chris. "We'd be gone while they fix it."

"It's only the seventh floor," said Bobby.

"Only!" cried Rob. *"Only!"* He stopped, momentarily speechless. "This is a *very big hotel!* The seventh floor has a lot of rooms. They'll have to examine them one by one—light fixture by light fixture!"

We all looked at each other. "I'll tell you what, Bobby," Rob said at last. "You take the damned lamp down to the front desk and tell them what happened."

"You mean . . . everything?" Bobby looked appalled. Rob hesitated. "Tell them you broke it. Maybe they won't ask how."

The boys left and Rob walked over to the window and looked out. "We can afford to pay for one lamp, I guess."

I joined him at the window and looked down on a city starting to wink with color. "Be glad, Rob. On a worse day Bobby could have blown out all the lights in Amsterdam."

That trip was a long time ago, and memory drops off, but I don't recall being asked to buy any lamps we didn't want.

THE BOYS DIDN'T ruin the trip, they just made it different. Our good days outnumbered the bad, both in quality and quantity. But the whole event had a breathtaking edge that other trips lacked.

Having found his smile again, Bobby came home partly restored, head no longer hanging, a brighter look to his face. He spoke in whole sentences. I wondered with a sort of giddy anticipation when we would travel to Europe with those two boys again.

As it turned out—never.

The boys found England quaint, and the Brits found the boys nerve-wracking.

The boys loved the scooters we rented on Mallorca.
Fortunately, no one stopped them to ask their ages.

Chapter Nine

Tracy and the Marine General

I WAS SITTING in the bleachers at a fancy swim club, waiting to watch our youngest kids compete in the Orange County swim finals, and I swear the whole thing was an accident. The fact that I was there at all. The fact that my kids were there. The fact that we had this reputation for being a family of jocks. Accident, accident, accident.

But then, I mused, *how accidental is most of life?*

For that matter, how unplanned and accidental was the core of my existence . . . my marriage?

Well . . . quite. More than I liked to admit. I began thinking back. For all Rob's energy, and his willingness back in our Stanford days to drive long distances to see me, his marriage proposal, when it came, showed a certain lack of advance planning. There was no bended knee, no diamond ring embedded in a cupcake, no "Will you marry me?" banner towed across the skies of Palo Alto—the kind of thing you read about because it takes rare masculine guts and always involves people you don't know.

Having vowed since early girlhood to be the centerpiece of a kind of courtship Fantasia, I found myself settling instead for a few careless words tossed out over a Caesar salad.

After Rob left me at Stanford and transferred to San Jose State, it was as though the lights went out at Palo Alto. Everything turned dim and less interesting, the classes paler, the studying more tedious. I remember how we hated saying good-bye after dates, and how Rob seemed forever behind the wheel of his stumpy green Turtle, driving, always driving.

One Saturday afternoon Rob and I were eating at Mannings Coffee Shop on Market Street in San Francisco. Around us, the clatter of dishes and hum of conversations provided constant background noise. In this setting that no one could have construed as romantic, Rob leaned across the Formica table and said earnestly, "You know, babe, I'm tired of running up and down Bayshore highway every night. I spend half my life in that car." As an afterthought he threw in a comment never intended to set me aflame. "We might as well get married."

There it was. All of it.

Perhaps I should have waited for more. Something bigger. Something closer to my dreams. Instead, my heart thumped in my throat and I gazed at him with a rush of warmth mixed with excitement, and I said at once, "Why don't we, Rob?"

He smiled. "We could, you know. With a little money from our folks, we could." And so it was decided.

He may not have meant his offhanded comment as a proposal, but he's never said he didn't—and anyway, three weeks later we were married.

Now, after decades of decision-making, I realize I gave infinitely more thought over the years to choosing our latest linoleum than I did to picking my life's companion. But somehow my instincts were right and it all worked out. And the warranty implied at Manning's Coffee Shop was good for a lifetime.

NOW HERE I was, about to watch Tracy, eight, and Kirk, six, compete in their first major swim meet . . . and I thought of the assorted accidents that had turned our family of six children into a cadre of determined athletes—all a bit strange when you consider that Rob and I were raised first and foremost as bookworms. As eggheads.

Our journey to the bleachers began because we had four boys and another child on the way, needed a larger house, and bought a half-acre lot that just happened to be a half-mile from a newly formed tennis club, which also happened to have three swimming pools. Neither Rob nor I wanted a backyard pool but, as I said to him, "The kids need something to do this summer," so I took them up to the club to swim.

Well, the Red Hill Tennis Club wasn't interested in having its junior members splashing around in its three pools. Oh, no. Certain mothers felt strongly that all children, even happy, frolicking children, had an inherent need to be organized. Before summer quite arrived, those mothers had formed the Red Hill Swim Team, and they'd dropped a net into the water and scooped up all the little splashers, even those who might have preferred cavorting around by themselves.

I remember how fast those Militant Mothers set upon me, and how quickly our kids were conscripted. "The Red Hill team needs your boys," the mothers said, "the team has a lot of empty slots." But of course. What other family could provide a child for every age group?

Voila! Suddenly our boys weren't just frolicking and splashing, they were flailing under the stern eyes of a swim coach and they were learning new strokes. They were racing. Which was fine with Rob, who swam well himself and always believed if there was any fractional bit of organized jock in his soul, the jock would have been a swimmer.

Not so me. Those first few swim meets seemed merely amusing. Splash, stroke, splash, touch the end, and the kid is out.

Then I began noticing that certain kids were *winning.* They were actually receiving blue ribbons for swimming faster than other kids. Like an infection, the first cells of competitive spirit clumped together in my psyche. Those little minnows were basking in praise, people actually cared how fast they swam. "By damn," I said to Rob, "if other kids can bring home ribbons, why not ours?"

"That's right," he echoed. "Why not?" Then he added without much thought, "Our kids must be as strong as any kids in that pool," neatly bypassing all considerations of technique and training. Suddenly the big feature was *winning*—which stuck out as the opposite of *losing.*

The disease took hold. By the end of summer I was full of competition fever, shouting at my kids like every other mother, exhorting them to win. Swimming—playing in the pool—was no longer a worthy goal and never would be again. All that poolside intensity had taken over my spirit, and I was a Swim Team Mother . . . forced into a modicum of decorum only because I once saw a mother run along the pool whipping a towel over her head, round and round as though her kid was a horse, and I never wanted to look like that.

Before our six children were grown, most became competitive swimmers, and one or another went on to become champions in five other sports: water polo, tennis, badminton, motorcycling and hang gliding. Even Rob and I had resorted to playing Saturday tennis as though it mattered, as though an engraved Wimbledon plate hung on the outcome. All those years, God forbid, a competitive jock had lain dormant inside the souls of two bookworms.

KIRK HAD ALREADY raced, winning a third and fifth, but Tracy was due to swim again. Rob and I felt good that the two had even qualified. For the last few weeks we'd seen plenty of commotion up at the Red Hill Tennis Club. As the big day approached, swim mothers turned hysterical, pacing the length of the pool as they followed their offspring with shrieking voices and clicking stopwatches.

Rob and I were never stopwatch parents; on the other hand, we never missed a meet. So now I sat next to Rob and waited for Tracy's second event.

At age eight, our daughter was all pixie haircut, bold new

teeth, and confident grin. She'd said almost nothing about her so-so finish in an early freestyle event, nor had Rob and I. In our family, mediocre finishers got a few consoling words and a lot of optimistic talk about future events.

Heaven knows we'd had enough practice over the years. You might say we'd become experts at dispensing false cheer and pretending that lost races didn't matter—when in fact they mattered quite a lot, at least for an hour or two.

That day Tracy didn't confide in us, so we didn't know what she was thinking. We were happy enough having her in the bleachers beside us, glad for whatever accidents had brought us to the moment. I suppose if I'd looked close I might have noticed a certain squared-up aspect to her that hadn't been there earlier. But I didn't. And Tracy never said, "I'm going to do better next time." She never said anything.

When it was time to swim her second and last event, the breaststroke, Tracy stood on the blocks, knees bent, tense and alert. At the gun she was like a stone in a slingshot. She flew into the pool with such fierce determination she began the race almost half a body length ahead of everyone else—an advantage so huge I assumed she'd false-started. But the referee's whistle never called them back, and Tracy never slowed. Nor did she glance sideways at her fellow swimmers. She simply pumped furiously with her arms and legs, bobbing and dipping, bobbing and dipping.

Before the lap was half over, she was yards ahead of the other little girls. When she touched the wall she was there by herself. She looked around expectantly, as though wondering what had happened to the others. Then the truth dawned on her, and she broke into a cheery grin that said, I guess I won.

As a matter of fact she did. She'd set a new Orange County age-group record that lasted for years, and she'd beaten not only all the girls but the boys' record, too.

She rejoined us in the stands, and after Rob and I had finished making a fuss and patting her on the rounded part of her bathing suit, she felt entitled to withdraw from her purse a giant purple sucker. Slowly she unwrapped the candy and was about to swipe her tongue over it like a heifer at a salt lick, when she happened to notice that imprinted on the back was the single word: "Winner."

"Look, Dad," she said, and Rob saw it and smiled.

Then a horrible thought occurred to him. "Is that all you get for winning? For God's sake, don't eat it!"

She ate it anyway.

TRACY WANDERED OFF and Rob I joked about the race. No child of ours had ever experienced such a startling unspoken epiphany—the moment when she thought to herself, *I may have lost the last race, but no way will I lose this one.*

"Eight years we've known her," said Rob, "and we've never seen that inner fire. She must have made up her mind she was going to touch first if she had to fly across the top of the water to do it."

I smiled. "That's about what she did."

LATER IN THE day, like a maraschino cherry on top, somebody decided that the visiting general from El Toro Marine Base would bestow the awards for that race. (All day he'd been referred to over the mike as "The General", which began to elevate him to pope-like importance.)

Intent on preserving the heady moment on film, Rob assigned me the still camera while he took movies. But from the moment "The General" approached the line of little girls, he presented a curious problem. The man stood close to six-foot-seven, and Tracy was about four-foot-three, and without a telephoto lens backed off at 50 yards, there was no way to compromise their two heads. Did we want a picture of the General's waist somewhere in the vicinity of Tracy's face? Or merely the General's head by itself?

Realizing the moment would be there and gone and possibly never photographed (for which I'd be forever disgraced), I kept squatting in front of the General and Tracy, and then jumping away to squat somewhere else, desperately trying to get a decent angle . . . while behind me, Rob was also jockeying. And while someone else did manage to get a reasonable picture of winner and presenter and give it to us, all Rob and I had to show for our efforts was one poorly focused picture of the General's middle juxtaposed to Tracy's face . . . and a lot of scrambled movie footage showing, among other things, the seat of my pants.

Tracy was large for her age, but so was the Marine General who presented her with the first-place medal in breaststroke.

Chapter Ten

It's a Teenage Thing

LIFE WAS SO much smoother when our kids were young . . . the river through our lives was placid and we seldom encountered rapids. Here were these obliging little people who actually wanted us around. At bedtime they hoped I'd read them *Winnie The Pooh* and ruffle their hair. They agreed that smoking was a bad thing to do, they thought Rob was funny enough to meet their friends, and they said things like, "You're coming to the school play, aren't you, Mom? I'm gonna be a cactus."

Then one day all that changed. Adolescent angst came rolling in on a wave of hormones. Rob and I acquired a mysterious taint, whatever is the opposite of pheromones, that made us unacceptable company in public. When someone like me showed up at school I was there merely to torture them, and my greeting was a protracted groan: "Oh, moth . . . errr." Our older kids clammed up and walled off their friends.

The angst befell some of our children more than others, but the most seriously afflicted was our third son, Eric, who decided one day that he *had* no parents.

Eric was about fourteen when he became an orphan. Wavy-haired, blue-eyed, and once sweet and affable, he was arguably the best-looking of our five sons—or at least the girls seemed to think so. They phoned him endlessly, and somehow, when I wasn't looking, Eric responded by disappearing. Where he went, or how, I never learned; I just knew he'd slipped away into some kind of mysterious netherworld that a mother could never enter . . . and odder still, a retreat that neither Rob nor I could locate.

To maintain the illusion of orphanhood, he went to astonishing lengths to avoid being seen out in the world with a mother. Eric would slither out side doors, hide among his tall friends, pretend he didn't know any female over twenty. He'd deny that he ever stood and waved to me from the kindergarten door, and in fact he was trying to create the impression that he'd arrived by a kind of reverse Immaculate Conception—via Joseph without Mary.

One day I tried to deliver lunch money to Eric at Foothill High school, and what he expected, I suppose, was my arm to appear by itself, proffer the money, and then fade away. He found my whole person such an unwelcome sight that as I approached the cafeteria he peered at me from behind a post like an edgy deer, as though prepared to bound away over the lunchroom tables. I could almost see the rapid exit of a well-formed rump. He wouldn't speak to me at all (his friends were there), but he did finally manage to whisper in the manner of Edgar Bergen so nobody could tell his lips were moving, "Please just *leave!* You're embarrassing me!"

This was the same boy whose teacher I'd tried to visit before class a few months earlier. Though Eric and I arrived together in the car—more or less—we were still a block from school when he cried, "Mom! Let me out here," and then, so nobody could possibly guess that he'd shared a vehicle with someone as objectionable as a mother, he hung back and slunk along at a fifty-yard distance as I walked toward his classroom.

When class started, Eric didn't show up. Though the teacher and I wanted a word with him, I had to admit to her that my presence eliminated any chance of *his* presence. "He just won't come in as long as I'm here," I said.

She smiled in sympathy. "Some of my teens do get a little strange." But on the way out the door I chanced to glance down a long corridor, and there at the end of it, peeping furtively around the corner, was a familiar head with wavy hair. The eyes watched me, the wary eyes of a wild creature, ready to spook at any threat of closer contact. The instant our glances met, the head ducked back and Eric disappeared.

Later I laughed. But at the moment I felt I'd acquired some kind of communicable disease, like Bubonic Plague, making it justifiable that a son like Eric would avoid me like . . . well, like the plague.

LITTLE KIDS ARE so wonderfully accommodating. For breakfast each morning I once gave my grammar school youngsters eggnogs. Back then I was a disciple of health food guru Adelle Davis, whose books I pored over as though she held the key to health's Holy Grail, and for whom protein was the *sine qua non* of nutrition. Thanks to Davis, I loaded those morning gruels (as Rob called them), with so much protein I probably sent my children off each day into wild, high-energy orbits. They were so over-proteined I doubt they ate much lunch. But as youngsters they never complained. You put enough chocolate powder into the thickest, eggiest drink and you can make a kid actually like it.

But then our older children became teenagers, and Chris swore I'd been putting things in their eggnogs I never did. I overheard him telling a friend, "She dumps in wheat germ and Brewer's yeast and egg shells."

Well, actually, he did see me adding shells once as a kind of calcium supplement, but then I reasoned the shells weren't designed to eat, but only to hold the egg . . . and besides, even I found the sandy texture unappealing.

For a few years, as youngsters, Chris, Bobby, and Eric were willing to drink carrot juice. Then came a teenage revolt with Eric declaring, "I'm never touching that yucky stuff again," and carrot juice vanished over the horizon and never reappeared. The younger kids didn't know what it was. But one day Tracy was complaining about her string beans and Bobby looked her in the eye and said, "Pipe down, Tracy. You never had to drink carrot juice."

As our children became teenagers, their willpowers surfaced and I could no longer placate them with a one-eggnog-fits-all. Suddenly I was catering to a rebel army, and my kitchen became more like Burger Max, where casseroles are anathema and the prevailing philosophy is that hamburgers are the only edible food.

Which wouldn't have been bad if the kids hadn't pushed their individuality, assuring that no two hamburgers came out the same. "You know I don't eat tomatoes," declared Bobby, "*Why* did you stick on tomatoes?"

"My hamburger's raw," said Eric.

"Mine isn't," said Chris. "It's way too dry."

I'd finally had enough. "You want it wet?" I snapped at Chris. "Go top it with ice cream. You can have hamburger a-la-mode."

Come to think of it, after the eggnogs, Chris probably didn't think that so strange.

IF INDIVIDUALITY IN food were limited to hamburgers, mealtime with teenagers might have been tolerable. But that wasn't the case. No two liked eggs cooked the same, or wanted the same pie at Christmas, or would tolerate the same ingredients in their casseroles. But then most of them didn't eat casseroles anyway. By the time they got through picking out all the items they didn't like, what was left on their plates was no longer a casserole. It was a collection of little piles of separate, discarded ingredients.

I accept the fact that during most of my kids' growing-up years I tried too hard—that I made a mistake long ago, when I began raising six only-children. I should have foreseen the consequences—that addressing each whim and quirk is impossible when it's one of you and six of them.

At times their whims turned maddening. The food issues were bad enough, but then they complained about their utensils. Chris said, "I keep telling you, Mom, I never eat cereal with a small spoon." Right then I was tempted to bounce the nearest small spoon off his head. Eric said, "How do you expect me to eat applesauce out of a flat dish?"

"I don't," I said. "Lap it up—like a cat!" In another second I'd be shouting.

THEN THERE WAS the matter of the opposite sex, a topic which ranked number one with our teenage girl and her friends, but was unknowable when it came to the boys—who might have been confiding in each other, but certainly never in us. Which is why the issue of imparting sex information to your sons is so laughable. When do you bring it up? For years they're too young and are entirely focused on baseball and soccer, and the subject would never match the topics in their heads. Before you've said a word you know you'd get nothing but blank stares or an embarrassed "Huh?" Besides, the boys have made it clear for years that girls are an abomination and beneath discussion.

And then one day they're too old and would rather discuss *anything* with Mom or Dad than their own sexuality. I'd look at one of my tall, muscular sons and think, *I'm going to talk to him about sex?*

Since I'd never had the nerve to bring up "that subject" with my sons, and they never discussed girls with me, all I could do was observe. Chris, at sixteen, apparently didn't know any girls, but whether he did or he didn't, he hated to be asked questions worse than Donald Rumsfeld.

Bobby, at seventeen, was so wrapped up in the heady fragrances and intriguing curves of his various engines that no girl could possibly compete.

There was hope for Eric, though he'd decided long ago that the source of all masculine charm lay in his long, curly, South-seas-island hair. The day I strong-armed him into getting a haircut, I wreaked more havoc on his self-esteem than Delilah did on Sampson. "I'm not going *anywhere,*" he declared with his arms folded across his chest. "I'm not leaving this house until my hair is back the way it was." Meaning thick and fluffy and draped like a blanket over his shoulders.

I was endlessly glad that Rob worked at capturing Eric on film before he reverted to his role as Prince Valiant.

TO MATCH THE peculiar behavior of our three teenagers, the younger three developed oddities of their own . . . and one ritual that became a yearly event. Starting about the middle of December, it popped up periodically until Christmas—namely, the re-labeling and re-allocating of already-purchased gifts.

The scenario became laughably predictable. The child who'd already bought a gift for one of his siblings imagined he'd earned a two-week license to hold it over the other's head. Call it seasonal blackmail. From that moment on, the recipient lost any right to anger the kid who'd been to the store. One misstep and the gift-giver howled, "Just for that, I'm taking back your present!" and he'd stomp over to the Christmas tree and haul out his box.

Sometimes such behavior backfired. "I don't care," snapped the other, "I've already taken *yours* back!"

We saw gifts assigned, taken back, and re-assigned three or four times before the Big Day—and more, if the kids were feeling especially war-like. After a while the labels got so smudged they were unreadable. On certain stormy days our Christmas tree was significant chiefly as a locale where the kids could store their brightly wrapped instruments of extortion.

But on Christmas things had a way of turning out all right. In the end the Spirit of the Season got to our children—yes, even ours—and each child received the gifts that were bought for him. Most years all turned out well.

But not always.

There was the Christmas that one of the older kids—Eric, probably—caught on to something I'd noticed a year or two earlier. With discarded wrappings still fresh in his lap, Eric held up a minimally scratched, slightly warped Arabian sword and stared at our fourth son, Kenny. "You didn't buy this, did you? Did you, Kenny?" He waited, and when his younger brother didn't answer,

Eric's tone grew more accusing. "You didn't get this at any store, did you?"

Grinning sheepishly, Kenny said, "I thought you liked swords and that kind of stuff." Clearly, Kenny had chosen to dodge Eric's accusations.

Eric tossed the sword back to him. "Yeah, I do like 'em—when they're not all bent and scratched."

Kenny retrieved his weapon and polished it on his sleeve. There was always next Christmas.

"I know where you got it," said Eric, pinning him with a look. "You got it out of your *bedroom!*"

Kenny didn't answer, but his silence was proof enough; he'd just revealed his favorite place to shop.

From then on, Christmas blackmail never worked especially well for Kenny.

Kenny's room was as shipshape as a space capsule.

Eric was at that age where everything he was interested in was illegal.

CHAPTER ELEVEN

Mad Hatter Inventors

WHEN YOU START having kids, you never say to your friends, "Now this is the son who's going to dig an underground fort and burrow across half the yard like the world's most determined mole . . . and this is the one who aspires to be a bird."

Somehow we saw our small children as surgeons-in-the-rough, or budding trial attorneys or incipient teachers, and it came as a surprise when one of them spent a large part of his youth looking for a way to launch himself into space, and another turned into an obsessive tunneler, then an inventor of crackpot vehicles, like motorized trash carts and hill-climbing rototillers. Far be it for Bobby to ride anything as mundane as an ordinary bike.

With six kids to keep track of, I didn't always know what the older boys were up to. I was so busy rushing out the door with a child to some lesson or other, and rushing back thirty minutes later so I could prepare to rush off again, that sometimes one or another of the kids could only get my attention by staggering into the house bleeding.

I was only half aware, therefore, that our second son, Chris, then 16, was determined to fly. Unlike the young male who leaps from the ridgepole of the barn with two garbage can lids affixed to his arms, Chris had loftier ambitions.

For weeks he labored feverishly out on the blacktop, mostly out of view, and it did not seem obvious from inside the house that he was building an airplane—until one day I came home from the grocery store to find something strange happening in my kitchen. As soon as I stepped inside I could see vapors rising toward the ceiling, making the kitchen mistier than a Scottish morning. A huge cooking pot sat on the stove, from which steam billowed out in mushroom clouds. Strips of wood protruded from the cauldron, and a fascinating tangle of strings ran from the wooden strips up to the handles of the kitchen cupboards.

I set down my bag of groceries with a thump.

Just then Chris ran into the kitchen and headed for the stove.

"What are you up to?" I asked. "What's in the pot? Some kind of knotty pine stew?"

He didn't seem to think the scene even slightly peculiar. "It's my plane," he said.

"Your airplane? You're *cooking* your airplane?"

"Yeah, kind of. I have to soften the wood so it'll be pliable, so I can bend it to form an airfoil. "

"And what are those strings?"

"Oh those." He leaned over the pot to make adjustments. "The strings keep the wood inside the steam."

"Oh." I said. "Yes." He was busy again, a surgeon tending to a patient whose leg was suspended from the ceiling. I was clearly the unnecessary person on the scene. "Well, then," I said, "try to take the cupboards out of traction by five, will you? I have to fix dinner."

The cooking-airplane scenario went on for a number of sessions, until one day when I was working in the garden the smell of something burning caught my attention. "Chris!" I yelled over to him, "you'd better go check the kitchen. It smells like you're barbecuing your plane."

Seconds later he ran outside with a long, smoking strand of string.

The cooking stopped, and days later he called me outside. "Come look, Mom."

I did, and there was his completed project.

"Wow!" I said. The skeletal wooden biplane that had been slowly growing under his hands was now covered with butcher paper and painted red.

"How do you like it, Mom?"

"I think it's great, Chris! It looks exactly like you hope it does. Like a plane."

"I modeled it after a German biplane. I'm calling it The Red Baron. So what do you think—should I paint a black Maltese cross on the top wing and tail?" Chris was one of the teens who still valued my opinion.

"Yes, sure. As long as it's not a swastika."

"They're different," he said, "not the same at all," offering my history lesson for the day. He stood back, sizing up his creation. "We're going to fly it next Saturday."

"How?" I peered closer; unless the missing element was stored elsewhere or it was actually there but transparent, the craft had no engine.

"It's a tow plane, Mom. Ram will pull me with my truck." Ramsey Price, 17, was Chris's best friend—and also Bobby's. "If we get it going fast enough, it should lift off the ground just fine." He never said what would happen next, and somehow I didn't think to ask. "Are you and Dad going to come watch?"

"Sure, Chris. You know we will."

ROB AND I arrived at a little-used street to find The Red Baron parked behind Chris's pickup. A large crowd, consisting of their friends and parents of friends, waited along the sides of the blacktop. The crowd murmured with anticipation as Chris and Ram secured a strong nylon rope to the back of the pickup, then to the plane, tying three knots on each end. It was easy to see that both boys were excited. Ramsey Price was six-two, with curly, light-brown hair and eyes that were brown like a cocker spaniel's, and he was grinning and moving rapidly from foot to foot. Crowds fired up his adrenaline.

"Look at this mob, Chris, we oughtta be doing something outrageous. Maybe you should try flying upside down."

Chris was tinkering with something inside. "I'll be happy enough if it works right side up."

The general mood was festive, with everyone waiting to be entertained. Nobody gave a thought to danger.

With the rope well knotted, Chris grabbed a leather helmet and pulled it down over his ears, and now he resembled one of those eager young German aviators, off to conquer the world for The Fatherland. Someone called out, "Where's your white scarf, Chris?"

Chris grinned and squeezed himself into the cockpit. Price scooted into the cab of the truck and started the engine, but at the last second Rob yelled, "Wait a minute!" and Price held up to let Rob and me climb into the truck's bed.

Rob shouted, "Tracy! Bring me the camera!" and she ran over and handed up his 8mm movie camera.

Ram began driving slowly, then faster and faster, and as Rob pointed the camera, we watched the plane roll down the street. Within seconds Chris and his plane left the ground.

The plane rose smoothly, and I thought, *My Lord, he's flying! Our crazy kid is actually airborne!*

But then Chris did something wrong, over controlled, he said later, and the plane dropped suddenly and smacked the pavement. Sparks flew out of the nose skid and the craft veered to one side. Ram screeched the truck to a halt.

With his usual patience, Chris climbed out of the craft and while everyone waited he attached a new skid.

"Next time, Price, drive faster," said Chris, and they worked out signals: thumbs up or thumbs down for more or less speed.

The second time, Price revved up the truck to their agreed-upon forty m.p.h., and the plane lifted off quickly and veered to the left. It was still rising when Chris worked the controls, trying to bank. Not knowing there'd be a delay, he banked more, and suddenly the plane was tipping precariously and in danger of going upside down. I thought Chris was going to crash.

I screamed.

Chris signaled with a series of frantic stabs: thumb down! Thumb down!

Just as it seemed he'd tip all the way over, the plane straightened of its own accord. Price slowed the truck, letting the line go slack.

Chris came down hard. But he was right side up.

The whole flight had lasted only seconds. Murmurs ran through the crowd, everyone talking about what had happened as though they'd witnessed a crash. People kept using the words "lucky escape."

There was no mention of a third flight. Ramsey Price was giving Chris a critique of his flying errors as the crowd began leaving.

After that it was generally assumed that the Red Baron was an obsolete craft—by everyone except Chris and Ram. They went out a few more times and Chris said he learned not to over control, but he gradually lost interest in a plane that could only fly at the end of a rope.

Eventually he put an ad in the paper and tried to sell the Red Baron for twenty-five dollars. People came to look. Some laughed and others thought it "interesting," but nobody was captivated enough to part with twenty-five dollars. Bobby offered to buy it, except he wanted it only five dollars' worth and Chris, in a burst of inventor's pride, said he wouldn't sell it for five dollars, he'd burn it first.

With all that paper and glue, the Red Baron made a spectacular bonfire.

CHRIS'S NEXT PLANE was an experimental aircraft, built for his senior-class project in high school. For this one, our neighbor, Leo Pfankuch, an aeronautical engineer, came over to help. With Pfankuch's advice, Chris began building a conventional airplane with a chrome moly frame and wooden wings. The biggest problem was that only Bobby knew how to weld, so Chris was forever waiting for his older brother (who was buried deep in other projects), to wrench himself loose. The next biggest problem was the wings, which consisted of thousands of small pieces of spruce, fitted and glued together like an endless jigsaw puzzle.

By the time Rob and I began paying real attention, Chris was three-quarters finished. He'd bought a used Volkswagen engine and was getting ready to cover the frame with cloth. Rob and I went out to the garage one day to take a look, and suddenly Rob was taking the craft seriously. "What are you going to do with this plane, Chris?"

Chris seemed to think the answer was obvious. "You know, Dad. Fly it."

"Fly it?" Rob shook his head. "I think we'd better talk about this. You don't have a pilot's license. You've never flown anything except the Red Baron."

"It'll be all right," said Chris, in the soothing tones of a vet stroking a nervous horse. "I'll take it out to the desert where nobody's around."

"Chris, you can't!" I cried, at the same instant Rob did a double take. Then we both moved closer, and Rob said, "It's not the people on the ground we're worried about."

Chris looked surprised. Apparently he'd never imagined we'd be *worried.* He thought a moment. "I know!" he said. Mr. Pfankuch can fly it! He's got a pilot's license." I could tell Chris considered our neighbor a second-best option, but at least better than nothing. "I'll fly it after he checks it out."

Rob shook his head. "Leo Pfankuch might not want to offer his life for your plane. It's possible he'll choose to live a while longer."

"I'll ask him."

"I'm sorry, Chris." Rob's regret was genuine. "I don't think this project will work."

Chris admitted later that he used his father as an excuse for giving up. But his real reasons were that summer was coming and Bobby wasn't helping and the project had become overwhelming. Besides, he'd already gotten an "A" in his high school class.

IT WASN'T ENOUGH that the area behind our garage had turned into a poor man's Boeing Aircraft. Bobby, too, had projects, but of an entirely different sort. Only later did I realize that Bobby's inventions reflected his offbeat sense of humor and that our oldest son was the quintessential maverick.

His crazy contraptions started with the motorized trash cart. The big, square, wooden platform on wheels was strictly intended for hauling trash to the curb—until Bobby put an engine on it. How he accomplished this, exactly, I was never quite sure, but I do remember his calling to all his younger siblings, "If you want a different kind of ride, come on out!"

With all his brothers and Tracy aboard, he chugged down our cul-de-sac street in bumpy, light-hearted triumph.

"Hold it right there!" Rob yelled the first time he saw the thing in motion. Moments later he dashed outside to take pictures as the trash cart rounded the curve with children hanging all over it, an octopus of flailing arms and legs dotted with grinning faces.

Then there was Bobby's hill-climbing rototiller, which he rode in elegant style, like a Rajah on an elephant, as it labored up a nearby slope.

Next he designed a souped-up hot rod that screamed like a 747 on takeoff and brought all our neighbors to their doors.

But the extravagant bicycles—those were his masterpieces. Young boys gathered from miles around to ride the sky-bike, which rose to nine feet on two triangular metal stems, perfect for a circus stunt rider, and his two double-deckers, which were marvels of cockeyed engineering. On the latter, the top-story man was eight feet off the ground and had his own handlebars, seat, and synchronized pedals.

Bobby was the only person I ever saw who could mount those elevated bicycle seats unaided. He made it look easy. Giving his bike a light push to get it rolling, he simply climbed up the assorted welded tubes until he reached the top. Even as he ascended, the machine continued to roll smoothly as if guided by an invisible hand. Though Chris assured us others could do it too, I saw only the failures, those who fell sideways, buried under a contraption the size of an oil rig—or the rest who resorted to propping the bike against the garage roof and crawling onto the seat under the eaves.

As Bobby and his friends pedaled down neighborhood streets they attracted endless double takes. Cars stopped, people waved, neighbors came out to watch. And sometimes Bobby came home with stories.

One day he reported that he'd been stopped by a policeman. "I thought he was going to give me a ticket," Bobby said. "I didn't know what for . . . but he didn't. He just said, 'I want to see how you get up on that thing,' so I got down and showed him. He watched me do it, then he shook his head and went back to his patrol car."

Behind all those projects—gadgets that pedaled, climbed, putted, chugged, and roared—Bobby was the moving force, the wizard of gizmo, always surrounded by neighborhood boys of all sizes, standing around in awe or begging for a ride.

(It was years later when a nurse said to Chris, "With all those boys in the family, you must have had a wild time growing up," and Chris said, "We did. Our friends didn't come over to play. They came over to watch.")

Even as he was living his cockeyed life at age nineteen, Bobby seemed to feel the same pressures as all over-scheduled Americans. One night I went out to the garage to try and shut him down. "It's midnight," I said, with my hand on the light switch, "please come to bed," and Bobby looked up and shook his head sadly. "The trouble with me is, I have too much to do. I never have enough time." I just looked at him. *Nobody's holding a gun to your head. These are your deadlines, Bobby.*

From time to time Rob tried to shut him down, too. He would stand at the edge of the garage, staring down at the accumulated mess scattered across the cement floor. The grease. The newly finished contraptions. The whacko pieces of half-finished projects, lying like beheaded toys that were killed before their time. Rob found it hard to accept what he saw—a nearly-grown son frittering away his days on whimsical inventions. "You've got to stop this,

Bobby. You're wasting your time out here." Frowning, he waved a dismayed hand across Bobby's artifacts. "None of this will amount to anything. Why don't you go back to school? Or go to work?" Rob's mainstream, mid-America values could not be submerged forever. "You're throwing your life away."

Bobby sat up straighter, newly indignant. "This isn't a waste of time, Dad. It's not. Something will come of this, you'll see. Just give me more time." He hovered protectively over the metal fenders propped between his knees and said more vehemently than he'd ever said before, "I don't *want* to do what everyone else does. I want to be *different!*"

Rob sighed and turned to leave. "You'd better figure out something else, Bobby. I'm not going to support you indefinitely."

As usual, the scene ended in a draw.

A FEW YEARS later, when writer Coles Phinizy came out from *Sports Illustrated* to interview our family for an article on yet another sport, he listened avidly as the family described Bobby's early days in the garage, spinning off one nutty invention after another. Coles Phinizy summed him up perfectly: "He was the neighborhood's most attractive nuisance."

We had our own Red Baron right at home.

A Nobel prize-winner stopped his speech mid-sentence when he saw this on the horizon.

Bobby was the king of contraptions, always good for double takes.

CHAPTER TWELVE

The Piano Recital

"THE BOYS, HERE, decided to go swimming."

The man who said it was glaring at Rob and me. He was an officer of sorts (by Rob's definition a Rent-a-Cop), he had three of our kids in custody, and he wasn't talking about the municipal plunge at midnight, or the city water supply, or somebody's private pool—he was referring to the large, statue-ornamented fountain that graced the entry to the Las Vegas Circus Circus Hotel.

We'd taken some of the kids for a few days' glitzy vacation (which Rob would do about once a week if he didn't have to work), and here were our boys—in trouble. It seemed that Chris, Kenny, and Kirk had chosen broad daylight to go wading for coins in the fountain—no doubt in part because Chris still remembered his trip to Europe and how he and Bobby had harvested coins from Scotland's Loch Katrine, and how thrilling it felt to fill your pockets with free money, some of which, like the old pennies, was huge.

Rob and I stared at the man and waited for the worst. We had learned of our boys' mischief a short time earlier when Tracy came running up to us as we walked toward the hotel. She was breathless with news, informing us a tad too gleefully that the boys were in Big Trouble and a policeman had taken them away and she knew where they were and we'd better come quick.

When we caught up with the boys they were huddled on chairs in the bowels of Circus Circus, sopping wet and towered over by this burly security guard with a marine haircut. The man seemed to be weighing his options—whether to ticket them or stuff them in the paddy wagon.

I, for one, didn't know what to say, as the kids already looked scared and wet and subdued, and this was such a rare state for them, I hated to disturb it. But the guard expected some sort of statement, so Rob began sternly, "I can see they've been swimming," and he gradually warmed to the task of bawling them out. "What were you guys thinking? Or were you thinking at all? Were you *trying* to spoil a good vacation? Getting yourselves hauled off to jail?"

Incredibly, the guard softened as Rob waxed more eloquent, perhaps because he now saw the miscreants as unlucky little fountain-splashers in serious peril from a grim and ruthless father.

By the end the guard saw us all in a different light. He said, "I'm a working man myself, and four kids is a bunch to take to Circus Circus." As though the kids were straight out of Dickens and all that bobbing in the fountain was their attempt to scrounge a few shillings for porridge.

After more of Rob's disciplinary words, the man's chiseled frown disappeared and he actually seemed on the verge of smiling. "Look folks, don't tell anybody, but I'll just let you go now," and he gave us a handful of free tickets for the circus and in we all went.

It was nice of him, but frankly I liked the boys better scared. Besides, the lesson was lost on them; they didn't learn a thing. We'd hardly arrived inside before Kenny, with an impudent grin, plunged his hand into his wet pocket and extracted a fistful of coins. "Look at this, Mom. He even let us keep the money."

WHILE OUR DAUGHTER seldom strayed into overt mischief, by age ten she showed a definite leaning toward excitement and activity, perhaps sampling a bit too freely from all the fine attractions life had to offer.

Tracy's piano teacher knew that her youngish pupil was trying to do too much—that she swam competitively, played age-group tennis, practiced cheerleading (for a non-existent audience), zoomed around the neighborhood on her bicycle, and was secretary of her elementary school. While Mrs. Cowan never suggested that Tracy ought to cut back, the teacher had been heard to say, with a sigh, that it would be nice if practicing the piano were closer to the top of Tracy's list.

After an all-too-memorable piano recital, Rob and I agreed that a greater emphasis on piano would definitely be a good thing.

The recital was held one Sunday evening in Mrs. Cowan's parlor, and Rob and I were there like all the other parents, dressed in church clothes and waiting anxiously to hear our progeny play the compositions they'd learned so painfully from memory. The young performers, too, were decked out in party dresses and little suits; we all took those recitals seriously. But Rob and I were realistic; we imagined Tracy would double-time her piece as usual—as though she had to get out of there fast because the piano bench was on fire.

As I recall, she was about seventh on the program, and before her, every child had done fine. Which is more than I can say for what came afterwards.

In the middle of her one and only piece, Tracy abruptly stopped playing and for a moment stared at the keys in confusion. The look on her face said she couldn't remember what came next.

But then she brightened and said, "Oh," and started over, giving a clear impression that she'd figured it out and the problem was solved.

The second time around she came to the same spot, paused a bit longer, said "Oh" again, and started over.

I had a sudden, unhappy premonition that this might not be the end. I could feel my jaw starting to clench.

The third time through Tracy said "Oh," now with an edge of real concern, and started over.

The fourth time she arrived at that same sticky spot and said "Oh," rather desperately . . . and what did she do? She started over.

By now Rob and I were feeling desperate ourselves, since it appeared that Tracy might go on murmuring "oh" and starting over for the rest of the evening. There wasn't a person in the room who didn't know every note in the first half of that composition by heart.

For some reason, Mrs. Cowan seemed loathe to interfere.

While I was contemplating a stealthy retreat out the front door and a quick walk home, Rob took charge. Standing up quietly, he walked the few steps and handed Tracy her piano book, which at least distracted the other parents and gave them something different to think about.

Tracy took the music and flipped it open to what I hoped was the second page. I certainly never wanted to hear the first half of that composition again.

For seconds she stared at the music intently, set her lips and . . . yes, she started over. But this time was different, you could feel her running at the piece like an old car determined to make it up a steep hill. In what seemed a miracle, she cleared the midpoint hurdle and kept going. With all of us frozen in stark, grim suspense, she chugged on, right through to the end. The relief among the other parents was palpable. You could sense them breathing again.

I was never in my life so glad to arrive at the end of a piece of music.

But Tracy had cast a dark spell over the program. She'd apparently created a musical rut that all the other kids fell into.

As though they'd caught some kind of recital disease, the next two girls and then a boy also got stuck, and like 78 records with scratches in the grooves, played their mistakes repetitiously until Mrs. Cowan quietly urged them to go on.

The disease worsened. Sour notes followed in other pieces. Then, to our amazement, the star performer finished the program with a triple-repeat. Afterwards, the teenage girl explained in all seriousness to Mrs. Cowan and the rest of us that one of the piano keys was acting up.

Well, if it was, Tracy did it. She simply wore it out starting over.

CHAPTER THIRTEEN

The Nash—by Chris Wills

IN HIS LATE teens, Chris and his friends had a thing about cars. Since I was not present for most of these events, they are best described in Chris's own words:

> My Grandpa Art loved Nash Ramblers. It was not because they were sexy or fast or stylish or plush. The Nash Rambler was none of the above. He loved them because they were cheap.
>
> Art grew up during the depression, and his early years were hard. As a child, my father's dad never had enough money for things we now consider necessities, like an extra pair of shoes or a change of clothes. Sometimes he and his four brothers didn't get enough to eat. As a result, even after he became a Commander in the Navy (having worked his way up through the ranks), Art was never able to get past his fear of being poor. It didn't matter that he finally had more than enough money for his needs, he was always looking for a "deal."
>
> I always thought the Nash Rambler was a particularly clunky design, with none of the styling features of the other modern cars in the 60's. It was fairly dependable, though, and the higher end models had some nice luxury features, but the car was basically ugly—and therefore the resale price was obscenely low. Which, of course, is why Art loved them.

As Bobby and I approached driving age, Art came over for visits, and inevitably he had a Nash ad from the newspaper tucked somewhere in his pocket. Art himself drove a Nash—he sometimes owned two or three—and he made a point of telling us what a bargain he'd gotten on his latest car. He always waited until an opportune time—when he was alone with us—and he'd pull out the ad and give us grandfatherly advice about how this car was such a good deal and how we'd be proud to own it when the time came to buy.

No matter how much he talked, Bobby and I still hated the Nash. It was old, it was ugly, and it was slow. The thing would certainly be an object of derision among our friends—we could hear them laughing without ever owning one—and it was a car that, in our opinion, made walking seem cool.

Bobby and I were always polite to Art and we dutifully took the ad and listened to his advice—and then threw away the clipping as soon as he left. In earlier years we'd tried to argue with him about how truly disgusting those cars were, but it finally became obvious that Art could not see beyond the wonderful price, so Bobby and I gave up.

Even after we got our driver's licenses and owned our own cars, Art still arrived in his Rambler with the requisite Nash ad.

Which is how we finally came to own one ourselves.

One day in 1969 during my junior year of high school, I was sitting at lunch with some friends, and I began emptying my pockets and found an ad that Art had given me days earlier for a Nash Rambler. I laughingly showed it to a few friends, and 'the plan' began to form.

This particular car was low mileage, it belonged to a private party, it had lots of options, and the advertised price was $25.00. We began tossing around the idea of putting up a few dollars, buying the car as a joint property thrasher, and destroying it for sheer pleasure.

As the day went on, the idea seemed better and better, and other friends eagerly joined 'the plan.' By evening we had eight firm promises and had gathered $5 each from our committed friends. Armed with $40 cash, we decided to buy the car and outfit it at Pep Boys with the best seatbelts money could buy. (Nash Ramblers did not have seatbelts—and we knew with what we had in mind for that car, we'd need them.)

We called on the ad, giving no hint of our intentions, and were assured by the owner that it was in excellent mechanical condition. Two friends and I got directions and set out.

The owner, about Art's age, was very proud of his car. He loved Nashes, had doted on the car for years, and was delighted to see that, for the first time he could recall, some young people had actually taken an interest in it. He wanted to give us all the mechanical details.

The three of us were not interested in the details, nor in any of his records, and we didn't want to test drive it either. We handed him the twenty-five dollars, cutting short his long-winded narrative. Without any attempt to negotiate, we asked for the keys.

The man was clearly flustered at our lack of interest in the finer points concerning his proud possession. The car was a dull, faded blue, an ugly beast like the rest of them, but he thought it was lovely and insisted on giving us the service records—which we took reluctantly without even glancing at them. We kept rushing him, trying to leave, and nearly got away without the pink slip. But he chased us down the driveway and stopped us to hand it over. "You boys will need this," he said as I rolled down the window. It was obvious he hadn't a clue about our underhanded plans for his pride and joy.

The minute we rounded the corner from his street, we stopped at a curbside garbage can (it was trash day), and threw out all the papers and the pink slip. They'd be of no use to us for this particular car. By the next day we had six seatbelts installed (very few cars at that time had more than two and most had none) and we were in business.

From that day on, the car was nearly always filled to capacity with kids, and was stored on any given night with whoever had it last. The keys were always left in the ignition, the doors were never locked, and in fact were seldom closed except when the car was in motion. The windows, of course, were perpetually open. Whenever any of us went to a store or restaurant or parking lot, we often left the engine running and the doors open—and the car was usually parked at an unusual attitude: straddling a curb or a cement parking stop.

This particular model had an unusual, pushbutton automatic

transmission, which was singularly handy for incurring abuse. At stoplights, for instance, our routine was to put the car in neutral, stomp on the brake, and then cycle the pushbuttons between drive and reverse with the engine floored and screaming. The rear wheels smoked and squealed and the rear of the car drifted left and then right, pivoting around the locked front wheels.

All the sane drivers around us became visibly nervous, and typically they inched forward or backward, whatever it took to get as far away as possible from our lunatic car and the lunatics inside.

We soon came to respect the off-road capabilities of that Nash. It is amazing what a car can do if you don't care what happens to it. The thing could jump curbs at 60 miles an hour with scant loss of control. Small trees, shrubs, and bushes had little effect on the front bumper. Even with sizeable jumps, the suspension seldom bottomed out.

Once, when Bobby took a shortcut over two curbs and a field at 50 mph, the front right wheel broke off. But the car made it home on three wheels and a brake drum, and because Nash parts were so cheap at the junkyard, we fixed it the next day for under five dollars. We also went through several sets of tires, but as always the junkyards kept us re-supplied for very little money.

The car did everything we wanted, and more, but we considered the big hill climb its finest achievement.

In an undeveloped area near our house, a 700-foot hill attracted all the local four-wheel-drive enthusiasts, who competed unofficially to see how far up the grade they could get. Very few reached the top. The rise was situated at the end of a street with a large curb, and the climb began about twenty feet past the curb and went nearly straight up. The whole thing was rough and rocky, with several areas where the soil was loose and chewed up from so many spinning wheels.

The usual routine was for the four-wheelers to ease over the curb, point themselves up the hill, and then creep in compound low straight up until they lost traction and had to slowly back down again. Some of the vehicles, which today would be called monster trucks, made the entire hill by virtue of brute horsepower and huge tires, but most had to settle for varying distances short of the top. Somebody had earlier placed stakes along one side, like mileage markers, and drivers could claim bragging rights according to how many stakes they passed.

Nobody tried the hill exactly like we did.

One day at school we sat around the lunch table wondering if the Nash could make the top. We decided right then its only hope was pure speed.

On the big test day we started a quarter mile down the road. With the engine floored, Bobby cycled through the automatic transmission gears, using the pushbuttons to hold lower gears until well past redline. When we finally hit the curb at the end of the street, we were going more than sixty, and were airborne for the entire distance from the curb to the beginning of the hill. The front bumper hit first, but fortunately at enough of an angle so that the impact pointed the car up the hill. With very little speed lost in the violent conversion from lateral motion to vertical, we were on our way.

Thanks to all the dirt sent aloft by the bumper, we lost all vision through the windshield. From that moment on we drove entirely from memory. The engine begged for mercy, the rear tires turned at an equivalent speed of 80 mph, and the dust was so thick breathing wasn't an option. By the crest of the hill our speed was down to less than five mph, but we'd made the top. Cool guys that we were, we drove away, not returning to acknowledge the cheers from all the four-wheelers and curious onlookers down below.

We soon discovered that our Nash could navigate most of the local off-road Jeep trails. We learned that the solution for any rough, difficult terrain was more speed. Occasionally we bogged down and had to be pulled out by a passing Jeep—but there were times when it worked the other way and we rescued one of them. All it took was a large rope tied to the bumper and an excessive amount of speed. The bumpers of that car were worthy of a tank; they could not be bent, let alone broken.

We were impressed with how long the car kept running. Although parts fell off in progressively larger numbers, causing a succession of minor traumas, the car refused to quit.

The Nash's end finally came—several months after we'd begun our systematic effort to destroy it. We were returning from the beach one Saturday with a full load of people (as was usually the case.) We happened to be halted at a stoplight in front of the exclusive Five Crowns restaurant on Pacific Coast Highway. Inside, the car was littered with all kinds of fast food trash, plus dirt and sand from the beach. Outside, it was caked in dirt and grime. The windows were smeared with mud and there were gaping holes in the upholstery.

The six of us were dutifully strapped into our seat belts and, as the engine screamed in protest, our driver alternated between drive and reverse, using the transmission pushbuttons and keeping the engine floored. By this time the motor was using an excessive amount of oil. An entire city block was filling with oil smoke from the exhaust—and tire smoke from the rear wheels. The cars behind us at the light had, as usual, all backed up a safe distance. Their drivers were undoubtedly convinced—and rightfully—that they had come upon a bunch of madmen.

Suddenly, with a final surge of reverse power, there was a huge bang from under the car and the entire drive shaft shot out to the left and traveled about fifty feet before coming to rest in a gutter. It was a final gift of dumb luck that no people or vehicles happened to be in its path. The drivers in the cars behind us were surely thinking, Serves them right. This will teach those idiots a lesson.

It was fairly obvious we were not going to be driving the car home that day. We all piled out of the Nash, laughing, and left the car running with the parking brake on. Without discussing our plans—everyone knew them—we left the doors open, kicked the fenders, and walked off down the highway to hitchhike home.

When last we saw the car, it was sitting in the intersection with a steady stream of smoke billowing out the exhaust pipe, the smell of burnt rubber permeating the air, and all the doors wide open. It still had about 10 gallons of gas and was running quite reliably, so it conceivably could have kept going for hours before the engine died. We never did know what finally happened to that car.

Many years later I learned that Art had found out about our Nash and what we'd done to it. He couldn't quite forgive us for destroying an automobile that offered so much value for so little money.

CHAPTER FOURTEEN

Eric's in the Kitchen with Dinah

QUITE OFTEN, WHEN Rob gets up in the morning, he asks, "What's the plan, Babe?" Though he's never said so, I think he privately hopes I'll produce some spectacular event for the day that will surprise and thrill him. "Didn't I tell you? Catherine Zeta-Jones is stopping by."

In our wildest days of raising kids, the plan never had to be stated. For Rob, each day's goal was to earn enough money to pay for what our passions had wrought, while avoiding as much as possible the subsequent confusion.

For me, things were simpler. In the early years, my goal was to get the last child into school so I could put on a red dress and go to town. When the day finally arrived, the house was so quiet it was shocking, and I didn't go to town after all, I went off to play tennis.

The kids grew and my goals changed. I watched in amazement as the older children went from zany to zanier, into ever higher orbits, and though I assumed I was making a difference in where they landed, now I think mostly I wasn't. Rob and I created the nest, but the birds flew where they wanted.

What could I do, then, but write it all down? What could I aspire to be, except an author?

Surely, I thought, *not everyone's kids are as offbeat as ours, there must be episodes in this family which would make people laugh.* So from time to time I wrote articles. Blindly. Optimistically. Expectantly. And sent them out.

Nobody bought them.

The writing flame flickered and dimmed, and my attention reverted to the birds crossing my line of vision.

What should we do about Eric? I wondered. He was about to be sent home from a distant private high school, yet he needed more discipline than I could offer.

"I think we have no choice," said Rob. "He'll have to go to my alma mater."

"You mean Army-Navy Academy—in Carlsbad?"

"Of course," he said. "I just hope they'll take him."

To our relief, they did.

ONE OF THE great moments in sending your son to a high-powered military school is catching your first glimpse of him, resplendent in his white uniform. There he stood, tall and straight in his long white jacket and creased trousers. How did they do it? Who would think it was possible to transform yesterday's slouch into this high-powered person who could play the lead in *An Officer And A Gentleman?*

Rob and I were dazzled. Right away, probably with our first sighting of Eric, Rob whipped out the camera. "Hold it right there, Eric. Head high. The sun is shining off your cap." Somehow we knew the dazzle couldn't last.

Another benefit, though we hadn't thought of it at the time, is that here in Southern California your spiffy new son might be hob-nobbing with some fairly high-profile teenagers, possibly even Hollywood kids, and who knows what adventures might rub off on you?

Which was exactly what happened.

It all began when Eric called home just after he'd arrived at the

Carlsbad Academy and said dryly, "My roommate's the son of a movie star. His dad is George Montgomery. Ever heard of him?"

Yes, I said, I'd heard of him. Eric seemed surprised; he evidently hadn't.

He added, "And his mother is Dinah . . . uh . . . well, she's a singer."

"You mean Dinah Shore?"

"Yeah, that's her. You know her, Mom?"

"I know of her. She's made lots of records."

"Oh. Then she must be famous."

"She certainly is. She even has her own TV show."

Long pause while Eric ruminated. "If she's so famous, how come I haven't heard of her?"

I said there were probably quite a few famous people he hadn't heard of.

"Her kid's okay, Mom. You wouldn't know . . . well, anything like *that,* just talking to him. He's pretty normal." And then after a meaningful pause, "Jody doesn't smoke."

That was Eric's bombshell, the tidbit intended to turn my knees weak with joy. Jody Montgomery wasn't a smoker. Wow. "Well that's good," I said, but without the intensity Eric expected, because frankly I hadn't sent him away to learn how to smoke.

"Jody may invite me to his place sometime."

"That would be nice, Eric. When?"

"I don't know. Probably soon."

I promptly dismissed our conversation. Not that it wasn't noteworthy, only that with Eric you wait and see. His inner vision of himself had always been unrealistic bordering on grandiose. According to Eric, he could make all A's next semester if he just set his mind to it; he'll probably be number one on the Academy tennis team the way he's been playing lately; and he'll soon be invited to a movie star's home. Only experience had taught us not to count on any of it.

At Christmas break, Eric announced as he walked in the door, "Jody Montgomery's going to invite me up to his house—you know, in Beverly Hills . . . " and with that he disappeared and was gone twelve hours, including when Jody called.

Somebody chalked up Jody's number on the board next to the phone, and later I said to the kids, "Do you realize we've got Dinah Shore's phone number on our blackboard?"

Chris said, "Don't get too excited, Mom. Jody probably has his own phone. Maybe his own house. I'll bet he never sees his mother."

Suddenly I had an image of Eric's poor rich roommate exiled over Christmas in his lonely room in the second house. Maybe it wasn't so wonderful, after all, being a movie star's kid.

Eric came home eventually and called the number, and it did turn out to be Dinah's number as well as Jody's, and before we knew it Eric was invited to Beverly Hills to spend a few days. What was more, we had to take him there!

As anyone knows, one adult with a car is more than sufficient for transporting one boy to Beverly Hills, even to a movie star's home. Offhand, I'd guess you wouldn't have to dress up. In lesser situations we'd been known to slow the car, push the kid out the door, and call as we drove away, "Phone us when you get bored."

This being what Eric was used to, he found to his slowly gathering amazement that the trip to Beverly Hills was turning into a red carpet event. In the first place, I told him to put on a decent shirt instead of a tee-shirt, which began to tip him off, and then I insisted he leave his beloved, bleach-speckled blue jeans at home. Furthermore, I said, he was not to take his dad's scruffy, Korean War army jacket.

Eric's look of surprise mutated into a frown.

Beyond such rigid and unreasonable requirements, he next discovered that not only were both parents coming ("We might meet her," I said to Rob), but one by one each of the younger children opted to go, until it seemed to Eric he would arrive in Beverly Hills with an entourage . . . trailed by the Tustin Hillbillies. Kirk had just declared, "And I'm going, too!" when Eric looked us all over incredulously, threw his jacket on the couch and wheeled out the door. "Then *I'm* not going!"

I had to drag him back.

After much muttering among ourselves, "Kirk, comb your hair," "What if the gate guard won't let us in?" we arrived at Dinah Shore's very modest home ("Hey, it's no bigger'n ours," said Kenny), behind the Beverly Hills Hotel.

We were in for a disappointment. Not only did we not meet Dinah (she was "busy" her secretary said), but Jody Montgomery came out to greet Eric wearing a pair of sorry-looking blue jeans and a scruffy tee-shirt. We asked if we could see his tennis court, and he said okay, though we were trailed through the house and out the back door by Eric, who kept hissing under his breath, "Why don't you just *leave?*"

TWO DAYS LATER, Eric called home about dinnertime. "Dinah wants me to stay another day so she can play tennis with Jody and me."

"You did get to see her, then?" I knew it was no use pumping him; Eric had a special knack for burying intriguing information in flat, colorless answers that you couldn't quite hear.

To my amazement he offered brightly that, sure he saw her, every day, and she was there with them now, having dinner in a Chinese restaurant—just Jody and Dinah and him. Furthermore, she was 'real nice,' he said. So, come get him tomorrow.

I said I would, and then on a sudden, wild impulse, envisioning Dinah playing English doubles with our two boys and in obvious need of a fourth, I blurted, "Go ask Dinah if she needs another player for tennis tomorrow. Tell her I'm not too bad."

Eric's usual response would have been an embarrassingly loud protest, followed—as he looked around to see who'd been looking—by a quiet but vehement No! . . . this hissed into the phone in the manner of a coded message delivered by a Russian spy.

But there was no such outburst, and I decided Dinah must have cast a spell on him, for he merely hesitated, and when I urged, "Go on, ask her," he did. Moments later he was back with a message. "She says be here at twelve o'clock. Lunch is at twelve-thirty. Tennis at one."

Oh my God, I thought, *imagine that!* But I couldn't let Eric know I'd just gone overboard as a star-struck groupie. "Okay," I said with forced calm. "Tell her I'll be there."

Now, lest anyone think I was childishly impressed by the invitation, like someone raised in the sticks—which I was—I did not call all my friends that day. I didn't tell anyone.

Okay, I was impressed. But I was also superstitious. When you've got magic in a box, you don't crack the lid prematurely and give it a chance to get away.

AFTER WORK, BEFORE I could reach Rob to tell him plans had changed, he drove to Beverly Hills to fetch Eric. Knowing my big match had probably evaporated, I went to bed in a funk.

To this day I have no idea what became of our mother-son foursome—maybe it never was—but as Rob explained after he arrived home and woke me at one in the morning, "You're playing tennis tomorrow with a bank president from Michigan who's out for the Rose Bowl game, and the Spanish Consul from Los Angeles. Eric's still there."

"Did you see Dinah?"

"Sure I saw her. I spent the whole evening with her. You'll like her, Babe. She's natural and unaffected, very gracious. You won't be nervous at all." He couldn't, however, vouch for the bank president or the Spanish Consul.

The next morning I prepared for the trip to Beverly Hills as though for the Academy Awards. Hair washed and set, tennis equipment counted three times, questions muttered aloud as I made the kids' breakfast, "I wonder what I should call her. Mrs. Montgomery? But she's not married to him any more. Miss Shore? That's kind of formal. Miss Dinah Shore? Dinah?"

Chris had heard enough. "Why don't you just call her Your Majesty?"

Suddenly I was out of time and had to jump in the car with curlers clinging to my head like damp spools of thread, and no recourse but to roll down the windows and dry my hair in freeway smog.

To my surprise, Dinah Shore opened the door herself, and I could see she was exactly as Rob had reported—warm, gracious, and natural. I asked, "Where are the boys?"

"They're off somewhere. They disappear and I never know where they go."

"That sounds exactly like Eric."

"It sounds like Jody, too," she said, and we laughed.

She led me in and I noticed how trim she looked in her cream-colored slacks. "You can change in that building," pointing to a little cottage near the pool. "I'll go put on my tennis things," and she disappeared.

I hurried into my tennis dress and then, still alone, I wandered around looking at Dinah's beautiful paintings, at her shelves of Emmys over the bar. All her furnishings were lovely, but nothing you'd be afraid to sit on.

The doorbell rang and I waited for the maid to come. When no maid appeared, I opened the door myself. It was the bank president and his wife—two cordial, mature people.

Presently Dinah joined us in her slim tennis dress, and then through the family room window we saw the Spanish Consul bounding around the corner of the house like a fleet-footed gazelle, cantering toward the tennis court.

As we went out the patio door, the Consul stopped abruptly. Turning, he wheeled toward Dinah with his face radiant and his arms outstretched, the quintessential adoring Spaniard. "Ah . . . Dinah! Dinah!" he said, and swept her hand up to his lips.

The rest of us were fascinated, but also relieved that he didn't offer to kiss anyone else.

The consul was a small, agile man, exceedingly trim, dark-haired and, for a tennis player, overly dapper. I didn't think he'd be much on the court.

To no one's surprise, the Spaniard paired himself with Dinah, leaving the banker for me. We took our places and I worried briefly about how I'd invited myself into this game, and what if I got so nervous I became a hopeless klutz?

What happened next wasn't so much nervousness as fate.

Dinah opened a new can of balls, handed two to the Spaniard then hit the third to me. I took a mighty swing, worthy of Muhammad Ali, but instead of connecting solidly I caught the ball on the frame and it whirled in startled circles before dropping at my feet. Then the errant ball began rolling across the court. As it headed for the open gate, I did a double-take and lurched after it. But too late. The ball managed to hold its lead and elude my grasping fingers.

To my horror, the escaping yellow orb ran down a little graveled path and straight into the swimming pool. And there it bobbed about like a rubber duck. Using my racket as a net, I leaned mightily and fished it out . . . and came back holding a dripping, worthless tennis ball.

What followed were a number of embarrassing minutes, as Dinah pondered out loud whether to send the gardener after another can, or merely put the wet one in the clothes dryer. The bank president wasn't too sure you could re-use a dunked ball, and the Spaniard didn't think the dryer would do it any good. The gardener wasn't near enough to summon easily, but finally the Spaniard decided we could slap the ball around a bit and it might dry eventually. (Eventually it did.)

From then on, I had a lot to atone for.

It turned out that the Consul, dapper or not, was a pro. He had great touch and deft moves, and while he ran the banker and me all over the court with his cuts and spins, he called out to Dinah between shots, "Your smile is dazzling."

She responded with a light laugh.

Another crafty, mean-spirited shot aimed at the banker and he turned to her and said, "Ah, Dinah! You are the sun that brightens a dark day."

She smiled again, now somewhat perfunctorily.

The Spaniard sent the ball into orbit with a shot neither the banker nor I could touch, and he blew his partner a kiss.

I couldn't believe his antics. While my partner and I were intent on watching the ball and trying to unwind the Spaniard's nasty spins—and also determined to treat our movie star like a normal person—the Spaniard was a whirling dervish of extravagant shots and corny compliments.

After a while Dinah's smile cooled, then froze.

"He's getting her rattled," I whispered to the banker, and he grinned broadly. Rattled or not, Dinah was a strong "B" player, while I, not bothered by a pesky sycophant for a partner, played at pretty much the same level.

But my biggest triumph that day was saving a second ball from escaping into the pool, this time with a Herculean dash that would have done credit to Florence Joyner.

After the third set we all stopped for lunch, set up on a folding table in the living room. Dinah asked if anybody wanted beer, and the Consul refused, but the banker and I said yes in unison.

Beer wasn't the only thing the Spaniard refused. He picked at his Mexican lunch like a dainty deer, nibbling at the lettuce leaves around the edges, and he kept talking about how he had another tennis date in a few minutes, this time with the famous Dorothy Bundy Cheney. I thought, *Next he'll claim to be paired up with Billy Jean King.* Presently he left, and Dinah said with a sly smile, "I really believe it is beneath a Spaniard's dignity to touch anything Mexican."

Later, when Dinah began talking about fixing black-eyed peas for New Year's Eve, the Michigan pair and I decided it was time to leave. I found Eric and persuaded Jody, who had some doubts, to come home with us, and we left Dinah in the kitchen with her honest-to-goodness black-eyed peas.

ALTHOUGH JODY WAS with us several weekends that year, we saw Dinah only once more—on Mother's Day down at the Academy. But that day, too, was memorable.

After the Mother's Day parade, Dinah invited Rob, Eric and me to have dinner with her family at the resort called La Costa—and at the last minute we all decided to throw in some tennis. Good enough, except that neither Rob nor I had the necessary equipment. That should have ended all talk of tennis, except that Dinah doesn't give up any easier than we do.

About then Rob remembered he had some old sweat pants and tennis shoes in the trunk.

"Good," said Dinah, throwing him her famous smile. "What about you, Maralys?"

"Eric has tennis shoes," I said. "I guess I can handle size twelve." I wasn't ready to admit that a man's twelve would only be two sizes too large.

"I can lend you a top," said Dinah, "and pants."

I looked at her petite size 4 figure, leagues away from mine. "Maybe the top," I said, and we headed for La Costa.

In Dinah's fancy resort room, Rob donned his wrinkled gray sweat pants and a t-shirt that said, "Haleiwa Strained Poi" in red letters on the back.

I slipped into Eric's floppy shoes, Dinah's skin-tight shirt (which fit me like a straitjacket), and over it Eric's white dress shirt intended to disguise the breast-squashing top. (Meanwhile Eric borrowed something of Jody's and they went off to do their own thing.) The three of us headed for the courts, with Dinah stopping the car to invite a couple of startled pedestrians to be our fourth. Nobody could, but it was fun seeing the surprise on their faces, the sudden grins.

This being Mother's Day, the courts were empty, and the pro shop tended by an aging elf who didn't know the merchandise. From him we bought me a pair of men's tennis shorts (he couldn't find any for women), rented two rackets, and borrowed a safety pin for the shorts. At that moment a male tennis player walked in.

Before he could say a word, the three of us pounced on him. "We need you for a fourth—how about it?" and the astonished man stared, then started to laugh. "Well, I'll be darned," he said. "I came here looking for a game but I didn't expect . . . this."

As it turned out, the man was exactly our level. We had two extremely close sets, ending the second set at nine-all, and nobody—not even me in Eric's big shoes and generous male shorts—was hindered by all the weird garb.

Afterwards we had dinner with Dinah, her daughter Missy, son-in-law Dave, Jody and Eric. The high point of my day was when Dinah invited a little old bald-headed man to dance, and he did . . . and the high point of Rob's day was when *he* danced with *her,* and the band broke into the theme song she'd sung in T.V. ads: "See the U.S.A. in your Chevrolet," and all the cooks and waiters came out to watch.

Being with a celebrity in public involves a whole world of new experiences, and how the celebrity handles it can tell you a great deal about her, and Rob and I agreed that by every measure Dinah Shore had to be one of the most down-to-earth people around.

Now we know why, years later, when Burt Reynolds was asked if he had any regrets in his life, he said he had only one—that he hadn't married Dinah Shore.

AS FOR ME, still yearning to craft offbeat family stories, the longer I knew Eric, the more I thought him worth writing about. Especially when I delved into his escapades with his best friend, Glenn.

Glenn was part of a mischievous theme that ran through Eric's life for all his growing-up years.

Eric's uniform wowed even his family.

Chapter Fifteen

Surfing the Swimming Pool

FOR SEVEN YEARS the Wills family had a karmic relationship with a family named Johnson. Though Rob and I genuinely liked the parents (they both had a keen sense of humor), and we saw them regularly at church and even went out to dinner occasionally as couples, what I didn't like about them was being called on so regularly to apologize.

The root of the problem was that, during most of their teens, our son and their son were best friends. In that amount of time I would have expected a sociable boy like Eric to have a number of different friends and spread his misdeeds around, so I could apologize to one family one week and another the next. But Eric seemed to have a special affinity for Glenn Johnson, starting with the day they built their first go-cart together. Or I should say *almost* built it, because when it came right down to putting on the last, needed touches, the Johnsons discovered that our two sons had commandeered the engine right off their brand new edger.

How was I to know that Eric and this boy I'd never met would choose to resurrect the old go-cart that had been rusting forever in a corner of our backyard? The thing had originally been Bobby's, then Chris's, but the older two had moved on to loftier projects and

I hadn't actually laid eyes on the aging cart for years, probably because it had languished out of sight behind a bush.

By the time I learned what was happening, the purloined engine was over at our house . . . and so was Glenn's mother, Jean. I remember finding her at our back door, where she introduced herself and explained with low-key courtesy that the boys' conscription of the Johnson engine to power the Wills go-cart simply wouldn't do. She gave me a rueful smile. "My husband found the edger lying on the patio like a gutted fish, stripped of all its vital organs."

I laughed and invited her in, but she said she didn't have time. "I just wanted to let you know we need our motor back."

The guilt which I keep handy for such occasions was right there, waiting. *She's being quite decent about this.*

"Of course," I said. "I'm sorry." As usual, Eric was operating in a mysterious netherworld, somewhere beyond my line of vision. "I had no idea what the boys were up to, Jean. But then that's nothing new with Eric."

"I'm afraid it's nothing new with Glenn, either. Well, tell Eric we're waiting. The edger may look unimportant to our kids, but to my husband it's a vital tool. He wasn't thrilled to find it torn apart before he'd even used it."

"What were they thinking?" I asked.

"Probably nothing. Do boys that age really think?"

We had a good laugh and became immediate friends. As events developed over the years, a strong friendship was needed to survive Eric's and Glenn's combined shenanigans.

Among other things, from their earliest get-togethers the two boys ran a private, interfamily swap meet, meaning they secretly traded possessions, which wouldn't have been alarming, except that every time Eric traded up Glenn traded down. Eric gave Glenn his ornamental Japanese sword, but Glenn gave away an expensive twenty-two rifle—which I learned about only after Jean called. "Please tell Eric to bring back Glenn's rifle. We'll be expecting him this afternoon—at which time he can pick up his sword." She didn't say 'fake sword'; she was too decent for that.

Eric gave Glenn some of Bobby's outdated English pennies (gathered from that loch in Scotland), in exchange for a couple of Glenn's rare Buffalo nickels. Glenn paid thirty dollars for Eric's surfboard with a "ding" in it (though for once Eric came out minus, having previously given a mini-bike for the surfboard.)

Here an explanation about Eric is needed. Our third son became an ardent opportunist in his early teens when he discovered it was possible to read magazine ads and send for manufacturers' free samples. For hours he pored over tiny print, clipping coupons and writing for freebies, even for things he didn't especially want, no doubt imagining that if he acquired enough of the world's goods for nothing he'd be incrementally richer than everyone else. I can still see him in a picture taken by Rob, sitting at the kitchen table with coupons strewn out all around him. Which all seemed fairly benign until he began trading with Glenn Johnson.

The boys' misadventures soon ranged beyond mere swapping. One night, for reasons none of the parents could fathom, they lobbed light bulbs at the home of their mutual girlfriend, Lisa. I suppose, to them, this was some kind of arcane courting ritual. However, to the girl, it was an underappreciated bit of mayhem. The bulbs exploded against the girl's window with a pop and a spray of glass shards . . . bringing an irate father to the door—and later, furious phone calls.

And I vividly recall a day early in the friendship when Glenn, who always seemed to come out on the bottom of every encounter, got the worst of it again.

It all began with Bobby, who came up with the wholly unreasonable notion that three boys could ride one bicycle down the steep road from our nearby tennis club without attracting disaster. (Naturally, none of this was communicated in advance to me.) Having persuaded Eric and Glenn to climb aboard and fit themselves two-deep on his one bicycle seat, Bobby sat on the crossbar and steered. As Eric explained later, "Bobby was the one who swore we could make the corner."

He swore wrong. The top of the hill went well enough, but the corner down below was strewn with loose sand, and the bike, already severely out of balance, couldn't execute the turn. Though Bobby tried valiantly to control it, the bike skidded, slid a considerable distance, and eventually fell on top of the two Wills boys, who in turn landed on top of Glenn.

The three of them dragged home as though from the Civil War. "Oh my Lord!" I cried as the boys staggered into the kitchen. "What were you *doing?" How did three of you get injured at once?*

The younger two glanced at Bobby, who had the grace to look chagrined. "Tell me later," I said. "Eric, go get the bathroom bucket." Among the three there was so much red raw flesh that the kitchen felt like a butcher shop. I didn't know where to start.

Bobby suffered a bad elbow scrape that was angry and scabby for weeks, and Eric had lesser abrasions on his arms. But Glenn hobbled around the kitchen with parts of him looking as though they'd been put through a hamburger grinder. Great patches of scarlet skin glistened on both elbows and both knees.

With buckets of water and a gallon of Phisohex, I sponged him off for an hour. Still, it took nerve to send him home like that to Jean and I was tempted to keep him until he healed. I really didn't want Jean calling with a new message: *Please return the rest of Glenn's body parts.*

After a couple of incidents like the light bulbs, it dawned on both families that it might be better for the two boys and everyone else if we discouraged their friendship.

We tried. Both sets of parents threatened and scolded. But still the two continued their errant ways. Together. One night, late, the two snuck over to Rob's parents' house, found Art's beloved Nash Rambler, rolled it silently out of the carport, and drove it all the way to Malibu. About dawn they returned the car, only to find their suspicious behavior had attracted a policeman, who pulled up behind them as they began to push the car back into the carport.

The cop shoved Eric up against the doors. "I don't suppose you took this car anywhere," he said.

"Oh no," the boys chorused together.

"Then how come the hood is smoking hot?"

The two boys were trying to worm out of it, stammering excuses, when Granny Ruth heard the commotion and flew outside. "Oh my stars!" she cried when she saw the policeman. Her hand went to her cheek and she seemed about to cry. "This is my car, officer. These are *good boys.* They're fine boys, they didn't mean any harm, they've never hurt anyone. Please, just let them go."

To everyone's surprise, the officer did. But then what policeman could resist the pleas of an emoting grandmother?

As Glenn said years later, "Granny Ruth was always right there, bailing us out."

Meanwhile Art was unaware that yet another Wills boy had been lured into mischief by the siren call of his marvelous Nash Rambler.

THE BOYS CONTINUED their forbidden friendship. But it wasn't until the pool incident that the Johnsons decided stronger measures were needed.

In a burst of ingenuity which seems to distinguish boys their age, or at least ours, Glenn and Eric decided one day to create a towing system that would allow them to surf across Glenn's backyard pool. For starters, Glenn would ride his surfboard inside the pool, while Eric rode his Vespa scooter outside, pulling Glenn as he went.

Their idea worked reasonably well until the surfboard hit a returning wave and balked. The sudden stop dragged both Eric and the Vespa off the cement apron and into an unexpected splash landing. For a short while it was a crowded pool—two surprised boys, a large surfboard and a drowning Vespa scooter.

As usual, Rob and I knew nothing about the failed surfing experiment until Glenn's father told us at church. "For two weeks, now," he finished grimly, "we've had an oil slick floating across the top of our swimming pool."

Oh God, I thought. Yet his dry words were all too visual and Rob and I couldn't stop laughing. "I'm . . . sorry," I said, but I was clearly choking on my apology.

By now the Johnson sense of humor had been tested to the limits.

The friendship hadn't done Eric any good, either. His grades at Foothill High had slipped, and we began to wonder if he'd even graduate. I made an appointment with the high school counselor, asking for the name of a good private school—somewhere far far from home. He suggested his own alma mater. So without telling the Johnsons, we started the enrollment process for Wasatch Academy, in Utah.

Soon afterwards, I ran into Jean at the grocery store. I still remember where we met—in Walker's Market over by the coolers of milk. I hadn't seen her in some time, and she said as she placed milk in her cart, "We're sending Glenn away to school. It's a fine, church-based boarding school recommended by our minister. We think it'll be just right for him. It's a long way from here and all the mischief he's been getting into." She didn't need to say, a long way from Eric. I knew.

"What a coincidence," I said with a smile. "We're sending Eric away too. His grades are terrible. He'll never finish high school if he doesn't start studying. The school counselor recommended a place in Utah."

Jean's expression changed; she looked positively stricken. "Utah!"

"Yes," I said. "A place called Wasatch Academy."

"Oh, no!" Jean's hands flew to her face, which had just turned the color of pewter.

"What's the matter?"

"You're not going to believe this . . ." She winced as she shook her head. "That's where we're sending Glenn!"

It was my turn to look stricken. There was no way to hide it; this simply wasn't possible. "You must be kidding, Jean."

"I wish I was."

We stared at each other. At the moment neither of us could summon the slightest bit of humor. "Why didn't one of us say something?" she said.

"I didn't think . . ." I began, "I never would have guessed . . ."

"Same problem with us," she said.

"It's not as if we talked to the same counselor . . ."

"I know." Her expression was a crazy mix of emotions. She was trying to smile and couldn't. But the same went for me; I was frankly horrified.

The implications were terrible. We both understood them perfectly, yet neither of us dared express them out loud. Was there some kind of strange psychic connection that decreed our sons would never escape one another?

I left the grocery store asking myself how, with all the thousands of schools available in this country, the Wills and Johnsons had managed to choose the same one. After all, the place wasn't Deerfield, it wasn't Exeter or Andover. It was Wasatch Academy in Mt. Pleasant, Utah. Until now, who'd ever heard of it?

I think, for the next month, each family expected the other to back out—maybe like a blind poker game. We'd already sent the money, so we felt committed, but Rob and I rather imagined the Johnsons would come up with a different alternative.

Yet they didn't. At church we made little jokes. "Well, at least Wasatch has lots of acreage," said Glenn's father. "I've told them to give Glenn his own building . . ."

"They'll probably be taking different classes," I said.

"Maybe they'll be tired of each other by then and go their separate ways," said Jean. We were all obviously stretching.

Somehow we'd started indulging the fiction that the boys were actually being separated.

As if we really believed this, the two families drove separately to Utah.

When we arrived we were hit with the final irony. Not only were our two sons not assigned different acres or different buildings—they were roommates! Johnson and Wills, corner room, first floor. The administrator said with perfect logic, "We thought they'd be happier, what with both of them coming from the same area." How could he know he was mixing gasoline and fire?

We may not have accomplished much that trip, but in the first ten minutes the Wills and the Johnsons hightailed it down to the office and made sure their boys were assigned to different floors.

For the next few months, all our important news about Eric came from Jean. Glenn wrote letters and Eric didn't. Glenn kept everyone informed about their mutual attitudes on the school, the food, and the state of their social life.

Eric wrote twice asking for money.

After a series of misadventures with the school administration—meaning they wouldn't put up with Eric leaving the campus without permission—he was sent home midyear. We popped him straight into the military school at Carlsbad, halfway to San Diego. He barely spent a night in his own bedroom.

Now, at last, the friends were truly separated.

The following spring, both boys graduated from their respective schools (Glenn with exceptionally fine grades, and Eric with some last-minute cramming that enabled him to pass), and the next summer, after Eric and I had our monumental face-off about haircuts and hair, Eric suddenly announced, "I'm going to go live with the Johnsons."

"Oh no, you're not," I said—though I had no idea where he *would* live. "I wouldn't think of doing that to Jean."

Eric went off in a huff, and an hour later he was back with Glenn. "I guess I'm not going to live with the Johnsons after all," he said cheerfully.

Well, I could have told you that. But I was curious enough to ask, "Why not?"

"His dad didn't go for the idea." Then he added, "Glenn's not going to live there either." It seems Glenn had spoken one word too many, and by mutual agreement was suddenly moving out.

Together, our two boys piled into a four-bedroom house nearby, rented by Bobby and three other displaced males. Eric was told he had to pay rent, but Glenn was given a scholarship. For providing "maid service" for six boys, he would live there free.

Shortly after they moved in together, Eric and Glenn began dating two Jewish girls. In spite of the fact that neither we nor the Johnsons had been able to get our sons more than passably interested in the Presbyterian Church, Eric told us one day, "Glenn and I are going to turn Jewish."

I just stared at him. And then I pictured the two of them wearing their yarmulkes, and I thought, *This is like the time they tried to surf the swimming pool. It'll never work.* And it didn't.

LATE THAT FIRST summer after graduation, the two boys headed for my mother's ranch in Mount Shasta, presumably to function as hired hands. As Glenn explained to me later, "Your mother wanted us to paint the barn—namely, she expected us to do real farm-type work. What we expected was a small amount of work and a large amount of time riding horses. One day we borrowed a shotgun and went down to the stream to shoot trout. We didn't hit any, but we did figure out how to move them around. Within a few hours we managed to collect a fair number of fish in one little pool. Somehow that wasn't part of our job description—herding trout. We only lasted on your mother's ranch one week."

Not long afterward they were home again, back to living with Bobby in his rented four-bedroom house.

BETWEEN THOSE BOYS, some patterns never changed. In their last few months of living together, Eric acquired several more possessions of Glenn's. He inherited Glenn's girlfriend, and he also acquired (for money), Glenn's oil-dripping Renault Dauphin which Rob dubbed "Smoky Pierre." "No matter what Eric paid for that car," Rob said later, "he made a bad deal." Shortly after the purchase Eric was unable to force Smoky Pierre to climb the tiny grade to our street, and finally the only way he could get home was to back up from whence he came and approach our neighborhood from another direction.

A few defunct trips later, Eric began negotiating with a junk dealer, whose price for Smoky Pierre, we guessed, would be negatively influenced by the fact that Eric would have to push it in.

A short time later I ran into Jean. She was shaking her head. "It's been a long, tough friendship, hasn't it?"

Yes, I said. "Remember when they took your edger apart?"

She laughed. "I hear the boys' neighbors have all signed a petition."

"A petition? A petition for what?"

"They want our boys out of the neighborhood." (After all those years I was still getting the news on Eric . . . from Jean.)

Later that week we saw the Johnsons at a church dinner. Glenn's father announced in gritty tones that he was expecting Eric to return his boat battery immediately.

A familiar embarrassment returned. "I didn't know Eric had it."

"Well he does. He's got it in Smoky Pierre."

"Oh." I couldn't believe what I was hearing. Another apology seemed called for—but somehow I couldn't muster it.

That night we phoned Eric.

"Yeah, I've got the battery," he said with some defiance. "I had to borrow it. How else can I drive that rotten old car into the junkyard?"

ERIC'S GONE NOW—but that's another story.

Not surprisingly, after all his good grades, Glenn Johnson became a lawyer. He married, has a daughter and a son, and lives in Costa Mesa, California. I presume those once-livid scars from Bobby's bicycle are no longer visible.

It is now the twenty-first century, and to my astonishment I learned recently that our two families are still entangled. Our son Chris, an orthopedic surgeon, sees Glenn the lawyer occasionally at social functions . . . and only last fall Glenn's son and Chris's son faced off against each other in the Division One CIF Championship water polo finals. The last shot fired in the game was Chris's son shooting against Glenn's son, who was the goalie.

If Glenn and Chris are smart, they'll make sure their two boys see each other only in the swimming pool. Letting them hang around anywhere else would invite the awakening of old karma—which could prove catastrophic.

Just thinking about it, though, raises feelings in me.

I miss Eric.

Chapter Sixteen

Surfing the Want Ads

ROB AND I have always operated on different planes: vague, dreamy, moonbeam goals do not interest him. All my small, failed attempts at selling stories did not suggest to him a future career, since he had yet to see Dollar One.

Instead he kept alluding to wives who raised children but also, mysteriously, brought home large paychecks. I never knew exactly who he was referring to.

BY 1972 ROB had said to me once too often, "Babe, it's time you earned some money. Some real money. You're one of the spenders in the family, you'd better become one of the earners—put your college degree to work. It's time you made a tangible contribution." As always, his topic lacked specificity. No mention of how much money he was thinking or where, exactly, I was supposed to get it.

The first few times I just stared at him, incredulous. I sensed that he thought my golden era had expired, that it was time to start making up for the twenty-three years in which I'd had it so soft and done practically nothing. I stood my ground and shook my head. *It's time you did something about your failing memory. You can't mean the twenty-three years we've just lived through.*

"Just what do you expect me to do?" I asked.

"Well, I don't know, Babe. Other women earn money, they find a way."

"Other women aren't raising six kids."

"You've only got three at home."

"Eric doesn't count, I suppose, now that he just eats here and brings his laundry."

He gave me *that look*; the look that said his patience was wearing thin. He said, "Figure it out, Babe. Women all over the world raise kids and earn money. Peasants in China carry their babies and plow the fields. You've been to college. So put your education to work."

"I'll have a job by tomorrow." *I'll go plow a field.*

After he departed for the world of gorgeous secretaries and lunches out, his words rang in my head—and so did all the arguments I'd had no chance to deliver.

If those years were so soft, how was it that I was the only resident adult who had enough courage to eat dinner with six children under the age of twelve? Instead, after work, Rob went to the gym in Long Beach, getting himself in good shape for something. I was never sure what.

If he'd dared show up occasionally at the dinner hour (instead of skipping right to the weekends), he'd have known that raising five boys and a girl was no one's idea of life at the Ritz. It was more like running a zoo with all the animals out of their cages, some hungry, some just mean. Even if you could stand the confusion, you could never shake the impression that one species was going to devour another.

I suspect Admiral Byrd would have chosen his trip to the South Pole over one of my trips to the grocery store, especially in the early days. At least life was orderly down there on the Pole. It either snowed or it didn't snow and the animals behaved predictably. Byrd wasn't trying to accomplish the impossible with five boys fighting over cookies in the back of the dog sled.

And consider the diapers. Just the diapers. If you multiply six kids times two and a half years, that's fifteen diaper-years, in which time even a mountain gorilla turns grey.

By 1972, of course, with the household roar reduced by half, it was possible to move around the house with no children clinging to my skirts, and often when I snuck away, mornings, you could find me on the tennis court. So I suppose it was true that as my muscles were getting harder, my work ethic was getting soft.

The last time Rob delivered his Chinese peasant/field plowing scenario, we were in bed. I was just falling asleep when he told me it was time to go to work. Of course that woke me right up. Work, Rob. Work. Right. I rolled over, trying to dismiss the whole dumb idea, but of course I couldn't; my mind jumped to full military alert, my army camouflage jacket was on, I was ready to fight back.

By then he was snoring.

There was no point in lying in bed any longer, conjuring up brilliant arguments against a man who had delivered his latest ultimatum and then gone off to sleep. Better to read the want ads and find out for sure whether I was hire-worthy or not. And we could all just forget my degree in psychology. Even UCLA would admit they never got calls from bosses panting to hire a graduate who'd earned twenty extra credits in the psych department.

With that in mind, I trundled out to the family room. It was two A.M. and the want ads were in the wastebasket where they belonged.

I turned on the oven to warm up the room, pulled the newspaper out of the trash, turned to "Jobs of Interest: Women" and settled down to find my new life.

But a problem presented itself immediately, a problem I was loathe to acknowledge, since until then I hadn't thought of myself as old. The want ads were printed so small I couldn't see to read them.

Either that, or the oven was giving off toxic fumes and putting my eyes out of focus. I hoped you could get blurred vision from gas, because who would hire someone who couldn't see well enough to read?

With the aid of a magnifying glass I found the beginning of the list and quickly learned that my college diploma, even buttressed by a teaching credential, did not prepare me for anything in the A's. Accounting. I could hardly account for the grocery money. Accounts-receivable. No better. I'd never managed to collect even the smallest debts in my own household. Assemblers. What did they assemble? Things I didn't understand, probably, electronic parts . . . and anyway, "must have exp."

Well then, the B's. Baby-sitters. God forbid: not until the sun goes dim and the oceans freeze solid. Barmaids. How badly did Rob want the money? Should I try for the one that said "mini skirt" or the more lenient, "no costume req." Could Rob even admit that his wife was a barmaid? Probably not.

On to Beauty Operator. Did this include haircuts? Because I still remembered the day I sent Rob off to law school with a home haircut so badly botched I was forced to fill in all the white, scalpy places with eyebrow pencil . . . which then found its way to his hands, ultimately producing black smudges in all his law books. Beauty operator had other drawbacks. Who wants to spend her days immersed in client soap operas, clucking over vile husbands who sneak their sexy, busty girlfriends off to the Bahamas?

Bookkeeper. Same problems as accounting.

Counter woman. Ah. There was one that fit my talents. It even said, "You'll be home by the time kiddies return from school." I was starting to copy the phone number when the words "Tastee Freeze" leapt out at me. That finished it. I would willingly scoop ice cream for hours, but never Tastee Freeze. I'd had too much of that goo spilled in my car. When the next job under Counter Woman turned out to be Jack In The Box, it was painfully obvious that familiarity does indeed breed contempt.

I supposed I could donate my college diploma to the school paper drive; that way it would be worth something.

Or perhaps I'd have to admit, finally, that somewhere buried in a drawer was that deliberately-forgotten teaching credential—which meant I could always return to the classroom. But frankly,

I'd hoped to avoid it. After twenty-three years spent mothering children, which I knew, even if Rob didn't, was a 24/7 occupation, I'd had dreams of doing something with adults.

Rob's final argument about working was that I was getting stale and needed to learn something new.

Okay, I thought, *You tell me, Rob old sport—what new thing can a mother of six possibly learn from a classroom full of children?*

For that matter, how much is there to know about Tastee Freeze?

THEN ONE DAY I decided again to become a writer.

I escaped in my car to a remote hill in nearby Lemon Heights, where I sat with a manual typewriter in my lap, pecking away, one slow sentence after another. This between bouts of dissecting the magically crafted words of *To Kill A Mockingbird.* At the end of two years I had a 350-page unsaleable manuscript. However, thanks to Harper Lee, I'd learned all the pretty nuances of using colons and semi-colons, and I could practically smell the mortar that holds scenes together.

I told Rob I'd found my new career.

But I was only guessing. I hoped and yearned, and carried sweet images of myself as a published author.

How was I to know it would take another year of sending out manuscripts before I earned my first penny . . . and five years after that before I earned what anyone would call "real pennies."

In the meanwhile, observing how busy I was at the typewriter, Rob stopped haranguing me to earn real money. I presume he was hoping for a miracle, just like I was.

CHAPTER SEVENTEEN

Up, Up and Oops!

AS USUAL, ROB and I were the last to know. Once more Chris was building a flying machine out on the blacktop, though no one would have guessed that rolls of clear plastic sheeting and bundles of bamboo from a lumber yard and small rolls of duct tape would have anything to do with aviation.

Chris's feverish approach to his work, however, and the constant, hovering presence of his friend Ramsey Price, and their frequent excited outbursts, should have been an automatic giveaway: the two fly-or-be-damned aviators were at it again.

This time the craft didn't *look* like a plane. Not even remotely. I stood near the back door studying Chris's latest creation. The big, translucent plastic sail was vaguely shaped like a diamond, while the open-framed box underneath resembled a monkey cage. The cage was fashioned from lengths of bamboo held together at the corners with gray duct tape. As I watched Chris and Ram layering on more tape, Bobby roared up our driveway on his thundering motorcycle. He dismounted carelessly and sauntered over to their project. "This what you've been working on, Chris?" He came over and felt the sail. "It looks like a beach umbrella."

"Well it's not," said Chris. "It's a hang glider,"

"How's it supposed to work?"

"You run down the hill and hang by your arms until it flies."

"That's all?"

Ram said, "What else do you want, Bobby?"

Leaning closer, Bobby grabbed the bamboo uprights and hoisted the craft into the air. He set it down again, frowning. "This thing weighs a ton. What makes you think it'll fly?"

"We saw a picture," said Chris.

Bobby laughed, and the other two looked irritated. None of them seemed to notice me; in a late-teens world, mothers hover between invisible and non-existent.

"You can laugh, Bobby," said Ram, "but the photo we saw was in the *National Geographic,* so you have to believe it. The guy there was flying a hang glider. The article didn't give any dimensions so we doped them out ourselves. We measured the man and figured he was about six feet tall. Then we measured the hang glider and did the math. You know . . . extrapolated."

Bobby turned away, smiling. "Too bad you're not flying a picture."

Privately, I agreed with Bobby.

But Chris didn't care what Bobby thought. Mentally, he was already flying.

FOR WEEKS CHRIS and Ram tried to get their beach umbrella to lift off. And for weeks the craft defied them. With Chris's bright, enthusiastic girlfriend, Betty-Jo, faithfully taking 8mm movies, Ram and Chris kept returning to the beach town of San Clemente, where they climbed a small hill that faced the ocean breeze and took turns sprinting down the slope under their craft, sometimes making small, experimental hops—all to no avail.

One Saturday, out of sheer curiosity, Bobby went out with them. We heard about it later, how Chris grabbed the hang glider as usual and loped down the hill, running into the ocean breeze. At the end he gave his customary little jump. "Did I fly, Bobby?" he called up to his brother.

"I saw you jump," said Bobby. "Do you mean is that flying? No, it's just jumping. Flying is when your feet leave the ground."

"Yeah. Well thanks," said Chris.

THE BREAKTHROUGH CAME when Chris decided at last that he no longer cared whether he fell and broke all his bones. That was the day he ran down the hill without reservation, ran without slowing, ran recklessly and all-out, as though there could be no danger, as though it was perfectly safe to throw oneself headlong down a slope under a craft made of saran wrap and chopsticks.

That day something happened. With more speed, the hang glider seemed to grow lighter, then gradually, lighter still. As the weight disappeared, Chris was able to churn his legs into greater and greater speeds. Finally he found himself doing a moon run, his feet brushing lightly over the ground but not really connected. And then his feet no longer touched earth at all. He skimmed down the hill, his legs dangling freely in space. He was up! He was flying!

Chris came home that night with his face aglow, so excited he was talking in exclamation points. "We did it, Dad! We left the ground!" He broke into a thousand-watt laugh. "Price and I made it happen. Our hang glider actually flew!" He seemed transformed, utterly caught up in his moment of flight. Soon Rob was laughing with him, and inside I was feeling all goosebumpy and trembly.

Ramsey Price was just as excited, his thoughts tumbling out one atop another, a virtual waterfall of words. "You can't hold back," he said, grinning madly. "You have to go for it, like you don't give a shit what happens. You have to pretend you don't care if you splat on the ground like a ripe melon."

"You going to come watch us, Mom?" Chris asked breathlessly. "Will you come out, Dad?"

"You know we will," I said. The splattered fruit image aside, I couldn't wait to see them actually fly. "How about next weekend?"

THE FOLLOWING SATURDAY, Rob and I went with them to San Clemente. There we saw Chris race down the hill under his plastic canopy, running with the intensity of an Olympic sprinter. Sooner than I expected, he lifted off and draped his arms over the bamboo cross bar. His feet kicked exuberantly in space and his face radiated so much joy I could almost feel the heat of it.

To my surprise, it wasn't a silent moment. The plastic rattled and crackled like a dozen bed sheets flapping in the wind . . . snap, crackle, snap, all the way to the bottom. Chris laughed aloud, and down below Ramsey Price hooted and yelled. As always, Betty-Jo stood off to one side and took movies.

"We can see why you like this," said Rob, waiting with me midway as Chris toted the hang glider back to where we stood.

"You landed so softly," I said. "I'm surprised."

"Yeah, I did," said Chris. "Isn't this the greatest?" His face was full of laughter. "Next week all my friends are coming. And Bobby's coming too."

The next week it was Bobby who flew (and sprained his ankle), and then Bobby who sat at the bottom of the hill for a few weeks, analyzing their landings. "I know why you guys aren't crashing," he said. "At the end you flare the kite, the way a seagull lands on the beach."

"I guess it's instinctive," said Chris. "You sort of tell yourself, 'I want to land now,' and that's when you pull back."

After his ankle healed, Bobby flew again, and from then on he was every bit as much the fly-or-die pilot as Chris.

Everyone who orbited around the three young aviators (including Rob and me), found their lives changed. "My chemistry professor came out and tried it," Chris reported back, "and he broke his leg. I really felt strange, watching him hobble into class."

A covey of friends tried the new sport and became part of the boys' flying adventures. Their pals, who hadn't been around for the learning part, saw only the go-for-it part, so they threw themselves down the hill without worrying, without reservation. Their crashes were spectacular. Like kamikaze pilots, they dove into the ground at full speed, or they flipped and landed with the hang glider on top of them.

"I've seen them dig furrows in the ground, and I've seen them plow right through cactus," said Chris, his grin as wide as his face. "The crashes have gotten to be the best part of flying."

Betty-Jo recorded it all on film, and later Chris exuberantly narrated her movies at parties.

But it was Bobby—bigger-and-better-Bobby—who moved the sport along by building a much larger bamboo and plastic hang glider. Now, with two kites rattling and crackling down the hill at San Clemente, crowds came out every Saturday and Sunday. Week by week the mobs grew until our intrepid pilots became the locals' weekend entertainment. For as long as the bamboo and plastic lasted, hang gliding had the crazy, exuberant, unprofessional look of man's first dabblings into aviation.

It was funny to watch, and Rob and I loved it.

FILLED WITH MY own newfound excitement, I went home and wrote articles. And suddenly I sold one to *United Airlines Mainliner Magazine.* The day the check came I screamed and yelled and called my friends and carried on.

"Well, Babe," said Rob with a smile, "you're off and running."

When the family traveled to Hawaii a month later, there was my article nesting in the seat pocket in front of me. It was all I could do not to grab the magazine and run up and down the aisle of the plane pointing to my special page.

Rob looked it over with a nod of satisfaction, and when he left the plane, he carried a half dozen magazines.

I had scarcely stopped celebrating before I sold another. And then others.

Our boys had made me an author!

INEVITABLY, HANG GLIDING changed. "We can't fly by our armpits anymore," Chris announced one day. "It's too tiring. And we're going too high."

With the assistance of Leo Pfankuch, the neighbor who'd helped Chris with earlier planes, the boys bought aluminum tubing and dacron, and Mr. Pfankuch hunkered down with them on our blacktop and helped create a new, more sophisticated hang glider.

"We've got a seat now," said Chris and I gathered that, compared to hanging by his armpits, this was like flying a Barcolounger. "We've got a control bar, too. We can change direction now and go wherever we want. The control bar makes it easy."

SUDDENLY THE BOYS sprouted grandiose ideas. Scary ideas. It was Bobby who came to Rob and announced, "Next weekend, Chris and I are going to fly off Saddleback Mountain."

He might as well have told Rob he was going to skydive without a parachute. "Saddleback Mountain!" Rob was thunderstruck and didn't mind saying so. "That mountain's a mile high!"

"We know," said Bobby, looking surprised, then anxious. He hadn't expected his father to react so vehemently. He scanned the room, and to his relief Chris ran in and the two took turns explaining to Rob that higher was actually safer, that you needed altitude to correct mistakes and set up landings. "Mistakes close to the ground—those are the dangerous ones," said Chris.

I stood by, listening. Not talking, just swept away. Fascinated. It was like watching a chess game with masters on both sides. Somehow I felt whoever won would be right. Rob would stop them if it wasn't safe. Or the boys would convince him if it was.

It was a strange moment, as though two new grownups had suddenly emerged in our family. Now, instead of two adults and six kids, we were four adults and four kids.

Our new adults won.

WHICH IS WHY Rob and I found ourselves, the next Saturday, standing some distance from Saddleback Mountain watching a speck form at the top of the sky. I stood there feeling nervous and exhilarated all at the same time.

As always, Bobby went first. Slowly the dot in the distance grew larger.

I grabbed the binoculars from Rob.

And then, gradually, the dot became a little blob.

Rob grabbed them back.

At last the blob changed again and became a hang glider. Toward the end a large, graceful bird with great yellow circles on its blue wings whooshed by over our heads. As though he'd been doing this all his life, Bobby landed sweetly, standing up. In the distance, the purplish mountain was still there, a thousand miles away.

As everyone rushed up to pound his shoulders, Bobby stood where he'd landed, nodding calmly as the onlookers exclaimed. Chris and Ram were exuberant; Bobby was merely satisfied.

As for me, I was amazed. Thrilled that he'd done it. Thrilled that I'd seen it. I thought Bobby was wonderful.

If I'd known anything at all, I would have been afraid.

HANG GLIDING EVOLVED at blistering speed into a worldwide sport. Young men made hang gliders in their garages. Then they rented empty shops and started businesses. New hang glider manufacturing companies popped up daily, proliferating like weeds.

Chris saw it all happening. One night in the fall of his junior year he came home from UCLA unexpectedly. "We have to get into the business ourselves, Dad. And we have to do it now."

Rob was startled. He was a lawyer, not a businessman, and he had no intention of becoming a hang glider manufacturer, even by proxy. "It's out of the question, Chris. You're the only one in the family who could possibly organize a new business, and you don't have the time." Considering the outrageous nature of Chris's proposal, Rob was surprisingly cool. "You're trying to get into medical school. A business would be a terrible distraction. It just won't work."

Chris had come prepared. He knew his father well and had his arguments ready.

Again I was fascinated. If this was the wrong move for our family, Rob would stop him. If it wasn't, Chris would prevail. I sat on the couch that evening, listening to them discuss it, saw Chris lose the first round. But gracefully. Chris always knew how to be graceful.

One night over the Christmas holidays Rob took us all out for cheeseburgers. Right there in Burger King, Chris brought up the subject again and somehow enticed Rob into naming the business we were never going to have. "Wills Wing," said Rob. "That's the perfect name."

Which is how Chris ultimately won. Once you have a name, how can you not have a business?

Nothing happened for a few months, but when it did, the change in our family was dramatic. Here we were once more, following where our children led.

Our first generation of hang gliders had no plans, no seat, no safety belt.

Bobby hits the target from over a mile high.

CHAPTER EIGHTEEN

Photographs Forever

FOR ANY ACTIVITY as new and dramatic as hang gliding, pictures were essential. Rob, always the family's keeper of the photographic flame, took few pictures of the sport himself, but ardently collected all dramatic shots taken by others . . . which was simply an extension of his role as family historian. Without Rob, many of our finest, funniest moments would have disappeared into the ether.

ROB HAS ALWAYS considered himself a master photographer. Over the years he has been inordinately fond of telling tourists as he offers to take their family snapshots, "I got an 'A' in photography."

He is not, however, moved to explain that the 'A' was literally in a different century, back when he was in Franklin Junior High School. He simply snaps the shots in good cheer and high spirits, and if their photos come out as well as most of ours, they probably believe that the stranger they met near the Grand Tetons was indeed singled out recently for his photographic prowess.

Such behavior comes naturally to Rob, who remembers every personal triumph, no matter how small or how ancient. He mentions often that he won the math medal in high school, and somewhat less often that he won a spelling bee in fourth grade, and he says without embarrassment, "I have a good memory for feats," (meaning those that involve him).

From the moment we became parents, Rob turned passionate about pictures. He devoted substantial portions of our everyday lives to capturing the family on film, and as the kids grew, so did his yen for preserving their activities. On every occasion part of his time was spent herding his flock of sheep into unnatural groupings, where he kept them pinned while he studied the background flora, the filtered light, the number of feet from the camera, and each and every facial expression—all the while talking as he fine-tuned: "Close in, gang. Squeeze together. Pictures are no good past seven feet." "Turn a little, the sun's up there!" "Hold your fish higher, Kenny." "Move left, Kirk, you've got a tree coming out of your head."

The passion carries him further. Rolls of half-exposed film are not allowed to repose in the camera, but must be shot out and finished, even if the last two frames are portraits of the garage door. Within 24 hours of his arrival home from a trip, Rob's first, most important errand out of the house, is always to Main Photo, where photos are never allowed to languish one day past development. Home again, the picture packet is off limits and cannot be opened before the master himself is ready to officiate—and certainly the photos can't be fingered. "Don't touch, Babe," he warns. "Don't handle them. You'll get them out of order!"

"I never get them out of order, Rob."

"Yes you do. I don't trust you."

"I've been keeping your pictures in order for years. I know how to do it. Now let's have a look."

"Your hands are dirty."

"They're not. I'm surgically scrubbed. I'll get rubber gloves."

"You'll see the pictures soon enough—when they're mounted."

We've had this conversation a thousand times. Finally my Germanic stubbornness surfaces and I push on to victory and a premature look at his cherished pictures—or I don't and give up with a disgusted sigh. At any rate, like a mortician, Rob will have the body available for viewing soon, because he'd rather stay up until two A.M. than leave his precious prints lying neglected in a Main Photo envelope.

To be fair, Rob is the only person I know who, like a scientist in pursuit of a germ, devotes hours to poring over tiny negatives with a magnifying glass, jotting down numbers and ordering reprints, addressing envelopes, and mailing off copies to all the people he took all that time to photograph.

For a man whose camera is an ordinary idiot-proof pop variety, who's never made a dime in photography nor entered a photography contest, his attention to the myriad details of picture taking mark him as a connoisseur, a professional without portfolio.

Which brings me to an annual ritual that reflects Rob's singular attitude and could stand as the mantra for the family: Memories fade and play tricks. If you don't leave behind your photograph, you weren't there and it didn't happen. In fact you've more or less lived for nothing.

THE NATURAL CULMINATION of Rob's ongoing drive to capture his family on film takes place each December, and is apt to become the second most noteworthy—or at least the most traumatic—event of the month.

For years Rob and I approached our Annual Family Picture with optimism assuming, falsely, that there had to be nothing to it. You assemble the group, you make them smile, you click the shutter. How hard can that be?

Very hard, as it turned out.

First and foremost we had to get everyone *there* . . . which, with eight people who were involved in tennis matches, swim meets, flying dates, motocross races, SAT tests and out-of-town universities, was like trying to assemble four hummingbirds, three minnows, and a cheetah.

Arranging the Yalta Summit, even throwing in Mussolini, would have been easier.

But second, there was the problem of dreaming up a setting, or theme, so we were not, as Rob said, "just standing there, like ducks in a row." And finally, since Rob could not tolerate even a hint that his family might appear ordinary or mundane, each year he gave us the same stern order, presented with all the formality of a bailiff ushering in the judge. "Everybody go find a hat."

Each year the task grew more difficult—until now, in the 21st Century, Rob must ambush his subjects and snap pictures whenever he can of those family members who happen to be within snapping range. Gone, or virtually gone, are pre-planned shots of the entire group.

Anyone with acuity would have recognized back in '73 that the Wills Yearly Picture was becoming obsolete and would soon go the way of the garter. But for nine years, at least, Rob had the fortitude to try, though it always took several weeks to bring all eight family members to a halt at once. Even so, there was always someone who said, "I can come, Dad, but I have to be at a tennis tournament by one," balanced, naturally, by the swimmer who declared he'd be in a swim meet all morning and couldn't arrive until 12:45.

As for the theme, it was difficult not to run out of them. If we'd all applied our brains to the situation, I'm sure we could have produced new themes indefinitely, but, as Rob said, "I am the *only one* who has thought about the problem at all." Which was true. The trouble with having a leader is that you learn over the years to let him lead.

However, once we were all assembled and Rob produced his theme, everybody started thinking hard, and all at once. "Do we *have* to have medals? I don't want to stand here holding a medal, like I'm bragging." "Up on the roof, Dad? Isn't that kind of dumb?" "Why in the garden? We've done the garden." Until Rob eventually exploded. "We're taking this picture and we're taking it now!" At which point we all ended up in the garden—or on the roof.

Some years the themes worked out well. The year we were on

the roof nobody minded, really. That is, nobody except the photographer. Since he felt in some peril of backing off the edge he was, understandably, glad to return to a surface without a tilt.

The time we posed everybody with their heads poking out the living-room casement windows would have been a happier occasion if the windows had been larger. As it was, the fellows on the bottom wanted the windows farther *up,* while those on top wanted them farther down. Rob finally placed the windows in the middle, assuring us that nobody would be decapitated. At that point the two cats, held by Tracy and Kirk, both elected to escape, and I remember how Kenny raced away to re-capture them, and how Rob said, "Everyone stay put until Kenny gets back," and how the minutes dragged on as I stood in the living room with my neck draped over the window frame, and how grateful I was that I wasn't Marie Antoinette.

One year we took our annual photo on the trampoline. That was the year Bobby shouted crossly, "Stop breathing so hard, Kenny, you're jiggling the rest of us." To make things worse, a fierce wind was blowing, and every few seconds the trampoline rebounded as someone dived after his escaping hat. Consequently that was the occasion Chris said, "There's only one way this'll work. Everyone has to put his hand on someone else's head."

Another year we assembled up and down our giant swing set. The boys who perched on the top pipe had nothing to hold on to and thus sat *very carefully,* with smiles frozen—but what did Rob expect? Why did he think they could sit there looking natural and easy when any minute they were apt to topple off?

Nineteen-seventy-three was Trophy Year. Everybody in the family won at least two that year, but when it came time to photograph the entire collection, carefully assembled by Rob on the patio, the general rebellion was so great that our leader finally succumbed. "You pick a theme," he growled at the group. This . . . after we'd waited an hour for Eric, who finally showed up just as it started to rain. "Umbrellas!" I cried. "We can all stand under umbrellas!"

Nobody rushed for the idea, and after two or three shots with nine people trying to squeeze under two umbrellas, we cast them aside and proceeded in the wet. Our recipients might have noticed that there was no theme that year. No hats ("Let's forget the hats!" said Chris), we were standing like ducks in a row, and everybody looked happy. Everybody except Rob.

We didn't know it then, but 1973 marked the end of our formal, pre-arranged Picture-of-the-Year.

It's not that we didn't take family pictures any more. We did. It's just that our family had changed. We no longer had everybody with us.

Rob would never settle for an orthodox family photo.

CHAPTER NINETEEN

The Tandem Flights

GIVEN A FIRST superficial glance, Chris never seemed as persistent as Bobby. He had none of Bobby's stern, solemn facial expressions, none of that relentless, pulling-the-dogsled approach to life. He was light and he was funny. He could always make me laugh.

Yet there was a hidden thread of steel buried deep in his personality. While outwardly, Chris was our merry whirlwind, the fact remained that he was also the prime mover in our family, the irresistible force that often won out over the immovable object. Nobody but Chris could have persuaded Rob, the conservative lawyer, to finance an upstart hang gliding company—face it, a business run by kids! Bobby couldn't have done it. I couldn't have done it. Nobody else would have thought to try.

But Chris, with his big grin and compelling logic—and of course with the endless enthusiasm that cascades out of him like an effervescent brook (and still does to this day), soon toppled Rob over the edge. And voila! by March of '73, the family had begun manufacturing hang gliders.

Chris made promises: "Eric will be our office manager, Dad. You know he needs something to do. And Bobby's a natural inventor, so he'll be the kite designer and test pilot. And I'll take a quarter off school to get everything started." His promises seemed so sweet.

"And who'll run this business when you go back to UCLA?" Rob asked.

"Eric," he said. "And Bobby. But I'll be checking in."

Rob believed him. But then everyone believes Chris.

Because I already had a title (mother), Chris did not propose a new life for me. Which meant I showed up when I got there, worked for no pay, and did a bit of everything. I wrote letters, answered the phone, sold kites, cleaned the bathroom, and picked aluminum filings out of the carpet. Nobody knew what to call me. So mostly they didn't call me anything.

As the only worker who was officially unofficial, it often fell to me to stay late and catch up on all the chores Eric and I hadn't finished. Occasionally I didn't arrive home until eight at night—by which time everyone in the family had eaten cereal for dinner, and everyone, including Rob, was whining and asking, "Where have you *been*?"

I sashayed through the kitchen, past their empty cereal bowls. "On a yacht, with Robert Redford. Where else?"

IN AUGUST, CHRIS married Betty-Jo, the fresh, town-and-country girl with an 8mm camera. How could he not marry the girl who'd so faithfully shadowed his adventures, who'd tromped the hills with him, who'd photographed his every move as though he deserved it, as though he'd been on loan from MGM?

Rob offered to send them to Hawaii on their honeymoon, but he also proposed that the rest of us catch up with them four days later.

I thought Chris and Betty-Jo would be horrified . . .

To my amazement, the two of them seemed pleased. And so we began a family tradition, accompanying our children on their honeymoons.

Such a honeymoon! After four golden days, the rest of us packed to go. Ignoring Rob's protests, Bobby insisted on loading two huge hang gliders atop the car. Watching irritably, Rob said, "Leave them home, Bobby. United Airlines will never let us bring those humongous things on board."

Bobby attached two bungee cords and drew them in tight. "Sure they will, Dad," he said cheerfully, "you'll see." And they did. Once Bobby and his big birds arrived, he and Chris spent parts of three days flying off mountains on Maui and Oahu, setting world records.

Still, it was Betty-Jo who earned the trophy nobody ever gave her: a solid gold, diamond-encrusted Good Sport of the Year award.

But Rob and I deserved some kind of award ourselves—maybe the stupidity medal—for letting Bobby talk us into the most outrageous act of our lives.

AT FIRST, BOBBY'S question seemed ridiculous. (In fact, even now it seems unthinkable.) Rob and I were reading in our rented house on Oahu when Bobby appeared and hovered over my chair. "Mom," he said, "why don't you and Dad fly tandem with me?"

I knew he was referring to the 1000-foot cliff above Sea Life Park—a cliff he'd only tried himself for the first time three days earlier.

He might as well have asked, "Why don't you and Dad sign up for an Apollo mission to the moon?" Even today I feel how it felt then, how I just looked at him in utter disbelief. He simply couldn't have imagined that *we*—his forty-four and forty-six year-old parents—would consider for one minute taking our first and only hang glider flight off that wind-blown, perilous cliff. Even Bobby couldn't be that disconnected.

He stood there gently making his case, while I, not listening, tried to tell him how it was. "Bobby, Bobby, this is me, your mother. I'm the world's biggest coward. I've ridden only one roller coaster in my life and I hated it. I never take chances. I detest drivers who speed. I ask people to let me out of their cars. Why then, why on earth, would I fly off a thousand-foot cliff? Even with you as the pilot?"

"You're not so old," he said gently. "I've taken lots of people tandem. Even grandmothers."

Because the whole idea still seems preposterous, because I now find it impossible to explain to anyone's satisfaction how Bobby summoned the arguments that made me change my mind, let me just say in my own defense: Bobby was amazing. In a different way than Chris, I honestly believe he was capable of making some of us do anything.

After I reluctantly agreed to fly with him, he grinned and said, "You'll be glad, Mom," and I shrugged and refused to dwell on it any further until we were on top of the cliff and he was setting up the hang glider.

MAYBE IT'S ENOUGH here to skim lightly over this event, though I did not skim lightly at all the day I flew. That day, for most of an hour, I was sheet-white with fear. To say I am a devout coward is an understatement akin to saying Rob lacks patience; it underplays how bad everything seemed. I had a sense of fatalism about that flight; for one reason or another, any reason out of dozens, I was going to die. I just knew it.

PICTURE US. BOBBY and I are sitting side-by-side on a narrow tandem seat the width of a Kleenex box. We have just launched from a cliff, and now we are hanging by what appear to be the yellow nylon ropes from a child's garden swing, positioned under a bright canopy with no more substance than a ladies' parasol.

We are two thousand feet off the ground.

I look down, though I can hardly bear to do it, and I see the earth spread out in a blushing purplish haze below me, and nothing appears normal, or even faintly reasonable. The people on the cliff I just left are invisible. For that matter, the cliff itself is almost invisible.

I can hardly breathe, I'm so terrified. Nothing holds me here on this tiny seat, nothing but the slenderest of seat belts across my lap. It is truly nothing. My feet dangle in space. I could faint and topple over backwards, and the seat belt would be useless. And so I cannot faint. I absolutely dare not faint. It is imperative at this moment that I remain conscious.

I feel my face going white. "Bobby," I say, because nobody should mention the word panic while dangling in space at two thousand feet, "Can we go down now?" My voice is a small, nervous squeak.

Bobby turns to look at me. "Why, Mom?" he asks in genuine surprise. "We just got here."

No we didn't, I'm thinking, *we've been up here forever, a thousand years, because even one minute is too long.* But I realize I cannot make my objections sound reasonable, so I sit frozen, trying not to jiggle those gossamer yellow threads that pretend to be ropes lest they somehow part from the sail. *If I don't move, maybe I won't weigh so much.*

Bobby is sensitive to my mood. "You'll be okay, Mom," he says solicitously. "Try to relax. It's smooth up here. Can't you tell how smooth it is?"

Well actually I can't, as I've never done this before.

"Look around," he says. "Look at that view! You can see everywhere."

You don't understand, Bobby, I don't care about the view! Anyway, I can't look around, it's too scary to look anywhere—down or off in the distance. I am blinded to all but my immediate environment, to the wind threatening to blow away my shoes, to my hands gripping the control bar. I sit motionless, struggling to think of some way to calm the terror. And then I notice something ghastly. Something beyond belief. I cry out to my son, "Bobby, there's a plane! And it's below us!"

He smiles. "Sure, Mom. Lots of 'em are below us."

"But that's not safe!" I exclaim, as though some part of this adventure might, after all, be safe.

"It is if you're not in their way," he says. "I can see, you know."

Well, that's good, I think, because I can't. Terror has frosted over my eyes.

Bobby becomes my host. "Look at those big waves! There, Mom, over there, that's Makapuu Beach." His arm is near my nose, pointing. "Do you see Makapuu?"

I turn my eyes an eighth of an inch, the sum total of all the movement I dare make, and catching a quick glimpse of ocean and waves, I nod, pretending that yes, it's Makapuu . . . though to me, from two thousand feet, all the waves and all the beaches look alike. Anyway, I can't forget where I am long enough to care which beach is which. In an airplane, with seat, seat belt, backrest, floor, walls, and windows I can study the coastline. Dangling by a thread above the clouds, I am not concerned with landmarks, I'm concerned with reaching the ground.

The minutes pass. I have endured this flight longer than I ever thought possible, and since I have not yet fallen off the seat, and since it's been forever since I last made my plea, I am willing to humble myself by bringing up an old tired subject. "Bobby, can we go down now?"

I hear my own thin voice and think, *Good heavens, I sound like a child.* Then I glance at his strong profile and think, *This is his world, and I am the child, and it's affected everything, even the way I speak to him.* How conversation changes when the roles are reversed!

"We're already headed down," Bobby says. "Look back, Mom. We're below the cliffs."

I look, and it's true. The cliffs now loom above us, which means we are less than a thousand feet off the ground, though it has happened without my noticing. Daring to glance below, I see that houses, trees, cars, the beach, have taken on near life-size proportions. I feel better, as though I am once more part of the planet.

Then even this changes and I feel more than better, in fact strangely euphoric, which is out of proportion to the sudden realization that I will probably survive after all. The feeling is joy, a wild, carefree kind of joy, and it bursts forth without warning. I realize I am experiencing something rare, living those moments of breathless flying we've all known only in dreams.

This is me! And I am flying!

Suddenly I can't get enough of it, the sensation of floating over tree and chimney alike, of feeling all-powerful, all magical. I am superhuman and I want to shout, Hey, everybody! Look up! Look up, I'm *flying!*

But it ends so quickly . . .

Suddenly we are over the beach and coming in fast.

In urgent tones Bobby issues instructions: "Listen, Mom. Push the bar out when I tell you." A pause. "Okay! Now!"

We move into a large, graceful turn, pushing together on the bar, though not very much. Abruptly the kite stops flying about four feet up and we hang momentarily, suspended as if by a giant hand holding up our kingpost. Then we drop on our bottoms in the sand.

"Sorry about that," Bobby murmurs, embarrassed. "I stalled kinda high."

From my sprawled position on the beach I look at him and smile. We were too high? Really? I hadn't noticed. We unbuckle our seat belts, and I pick myself off the sand and brush at my clothes. Then, without knowing I am going to do it, I throw my arms around Bobby and hug him. Words pour out, a whole flood of words. "You were wonderful, Bobby, incredible, the best."

He draws back and gives me a strange look.

"Thanks for taking me. You were right to talk me into it. I'm glad I went, I wouldn't have missed it for the world." I am babbling out of control.

He stares at me now, incredulous. All this coming from someone who moments before had been speechless with fear, begging to come down. Absently he pats my shoulder. "Yeah, Mom," he mumbles, "you're welcome." Then he begins folding up the kite, but over his shoulder he keeps stealing little puzzled looks.

The odd thing is, I mean every word. He'd been terrific. The definitive pilot. A master. The experience has been a highlight of my life. Because of him I've accomplished the unthinkable, lived through unbearable panic and survived with most of my dignity intact. It is an experience few people like me will ever have, and I am insanely grateful to be one of the few.

One last thought lingers in my head, though, an idea I dare not express, which Bobby will never know as long as we both shall live. I've done it and I am glad.

But now I never have to do it again!

THOUGH I BEGGED Bobby there on the beach, "Please don't take Dad. He says he's squeamish about heights—but actually, he's scared stiff," Bobby ignored me and an hour later persuaded Rob to take his own tandem flight.

I could have killed Rob for agreeing; I was sure he'd keel over with an airborne heart attack and destroy them both. But then, fickle man that he is, he went yahooing through the sky, loving every minute.

So then I was ready to kill him for being so unpredictable.

I SAW BOBBY in a new light after that—he seemed older, infinitely more mature. Our relationship shifted subtly, from mother-son to just friends, and I doubted I'd ever tell him what to do again. Which must be what happens when you hand one of your kids responsibility for your life.

Rob decided if Maralys can soar in Hawaii, so can he.

CHAPTER TWENTY

Murray Tanner's Flying Lesson

THE SPORT OF hang gliding changed Bobby more than it changed the rest of us, but maybe that was because Bobby had farther to go.

Bobby was the child who never quite meshed with the rest of the family, he was the one who drummed out of sync, tapping an off-rhythm beat to all the other drummers. But Bobby didn't care. All those arguments he'd had with Rob about leaving the garage and finding a life seemed to pass over Bobby's head as if Rob had never spoken. And his cry never varied. "I want to be different! Why should I spend my life doing stuff other people have already done? What's the point of that? I'm going to do things that have never been done before."

Sometimes Rob had snorted in disgust, and other times he struggled to find patience. He hadn't understood his son, but he meant to try. "What different things, exactly, are you talking about?" Rob asked.

Bobby never knew.

"Well, you'd better go to college," said Rob. "Or find a job. You can't just sit here doing nothing."

"This isn't nothing!" Bobby always cried. "It's important."

Before the hang gliding, I'd heard those conversations and

despaired, wondering which horizons Bobby ought to be seeking. *What is left in this world,* I mused, *that hasn't already been done?*

How were we to know that it would be Chris, our flying-mad son, who would bring Bobby the "different" life he craved so desperately?

Every day in 1973—thanks to Chris—Bobby was doing something that had never been done before. He was the first person to fly a hang glider hanging by his knees. He was the first pilot to take up a passenger. He was the first adventurer to soar a hang glider off the 1000-foot cliff in Oahu.

And then Bobby went a little nuts. He was the only pilot anyone ever heard of (before or since), to carry six people on one hang glider. Like the time he'd disastrously stuffed three kids onto one bicycle, Bobby loaded up his hang glider with five intrepid souls swinging from the control bar and each other.

Only this time, by some miracle, it wasn't a disaster.

Someone took movies, and someone else narrated the film. The audience sees an over-loaded kite skimming down a hill with people hanging all over it like laundry. A solemn, masculine voice intones, "Bobby Wills runs the world's smallest airline. It has a pilot, a co-pilot, a stewardess and three passengers. On Bobby's airline, the stronger your grip, the longer your trip."

Bobby soon became famous, known internationally because he was always entering competitions and winning. Within a few years he'd become the hang gliding champion of Canada, the United States, and Great Britain, and people scratched and fought to get a moment of his time.

Yet in some ways Bobby gave time freely. For his friends, our son was never short of time. Whatever Bobby could do, he imagined his pals could do as well.

But there was more to it than Bobby's blind faith that anyone could do anything if he just put his mind to it. Bobby loved flying with a passion that transcended even his earlier dedication to oddball contraptions. He loved the freedom of soaring, reveled in the sensation of moving his body through endless space. He loved flying the way a poet loves words, for the moment-by-moment sensations: the sheer beauty of unfettered motion, the mystique of birdlike maneuvers.

Flying so captivated Bobby that he was driven to bring everyone else along. And that included a graying fifty-year-old whom Bobby viewed as a contemporary, age being an incidental factor.

"Mom, you've got to meet Murray Tanner," Bobby said to me one day. "Tomorrow I'm giving him a flying lesson. His wife's coming and I know you'll like her. Why don't you come out to the hill and watch?"

And so the next day I found myself posted on a weed-covered slope, smiling at his friend, Murray, whose silvery, marine-cut hair said he was thirty years older than Bobby, but whose slight body could have been any age. Murray took me aside, eager to tell me all about our oldest. "I thought my son was doing crazy stuff, but Bobby has him beat by a mile. He's even got me flying—such as it is!"

"Hey, Murray—" Bobby came up and clapped the older man on the shoulder, "You're going to be a *good* pilot!" Behind Bobby, other pilots were setting up their kites.

Lois Tanner walked up and Bobby introduced her, a perky woman who radiated energy and good spirits. "We've all been wondering what you're like," she said. *We must meet this peculiar mother that raised such an offbeat son.* I smiled. *As you can see, I'm perfectly normal.*

As Bobby started up the hill, gesturing for his friend to follow, Murray leaned toward me and raised his brows. "Lois thinks I'm nuts to be doing this at my age. But when Bobby gets an idea in his head you can't bust it loose. And . . . " he shrugged, "here I am. Pretending I'm a kid."

Murray followed Bobby part way up the slope and then stood like a patient child, letting Bobby strap him into a hang glider. We could hear Bobby's instructions. "Get the seat belt good and tight, Murray, and remember, don't jump at the kite. You have to be flying before you sit."

Standing beside me, Lois pointed at the hill. "How's he going to run in all those weeds?"

I didn't know, but I agreed that Murray had a problem. The hill was covered in dense growth, like a mature barley crop, and I wondered why Bobby had brought us to such a weedy slope when he knew all the hills around like a deer.

Murray, however, seemed unconcerned, and listened dutifully to his mentor's instructions.

With a final, careful inspection of the kite, Bobby placed his hands over the older man's, guided the sail to a slightly different angle, and backed off shouting, "Go, Murray! Run! Run!"

Murray took off, and Lois and I watched with a certain lack of optimism. Around us, the other flyers had stopped to observe, as though Murray was a special case, which among all those younger pilots, he was.

Bobby's friend ran valiantly, but being short, he couldn't gain anything like enough speed with his legs tangled in weeds. After he'd stumbled and tripped about as long as his good nature allowed, he bypassed Bobby's admonitions and jumped at the kite (sat down on the swing seat), and waited hopefully for his craft to fly.

Bobby shouted, "You can't do that, Murray!"

Even I knew this should have ensured the end of the flight. But because the hill was steep and the kite had gathered some air speed, the craft responded momentarily and Murray became airborne.

However, the kite couldn't compensate long for Murray's mistake. Knowing his flight was about to end, Murray threw the control bar forward, gained a slight amount of additional altitude, and put the craft into a stall.

Bobby shouted, "No, Murray! No!" But his pupil was too busy to listen.

Even to Murray it was obvious that the stall was wrong, so he corrected by pulling the nose down sharply—which of course put him into an immediate dive. He overcorrected again and that's how he progressed down the hill—up, down, up, down, like a porpoise breaking through the waves.

Bobby stood transfixed, unable to believe what was happening.

Murray was now so far down the hill that all we could see of him was the top of his sail undulating above the weeds. I thought maybe he'd make it to the bottom.

Not so. Without warning, the dipping and bobbing of his sail stopped and Murray Tanner gently disappeared.

Bobby ran down the hill to Murray's rescue.

None of us had ever seen this happen before, a man and his hang glider buried so deep in an ocean of weeds that he was entirely out of sight. But you had to agree the weeds made for a soft landing.

Fascinated, Lois and I stared down the hill. After a while Murray Tanner rose up out of the weeds like a turtle coming up for air. His kite was neatly folded and he had a look of benign satisfaction.

Bobby came up to him, laughing. He hoisted the kite onto his own shoulders and let Murray follow him up the hill. As they came closer, we heard Bobby say, "We couldn't see you, Murray, but we knew you were doing *something* down there . . . pretty neat, getting the kite all folded." Then Bobby added, "You over controlled, Murray."

"Thought so."

"You *knew* you were doing it?"

"Well, it felt like it, but then I couldn't see too well on account of all those weeds."

"You wouldn't have been near the weeds, Murray, if you hadn't jumped at the kite."

"That so?" said Murray. "Guess I'll have to try it again."

"Maybe if we start farther up the hill," Bobby offered, "higher, where it's not so thick." He rubbed his chin, considering. "Of course you have it pretty well trampled down now . . ." and indeed, Murray had leveled a fairly wide swath.

"Higher sounds like a practical idea," said Murray.

So Bobby took his friend farther up the hill, and Lois and I murmured to each other that now *everybody* would fly, but nobody did. Murray, it seemed, had long since become a hillside phenomenon, unpredictable at the very least, and nobody wanted to miss the show.

Once on smoother terrain, Bobby talked to Murray like a patient coach, and then he launched the older man again, this time bellowing, "RUN, MURRAY! RUN!" as if the very loudness of his voice would kindle speed in Murray's legs. And perhaps his yelling did make a difference, because this time Murray Tanner became airborne in a hurry and passed us some twenty feet over our heads and going higher.

Satisfied, Bobby nodded. And Murray, too, seemed inordinately pleased as he flew by. His small frame was snugged into the swing seat and his legs crossed at the ankles, like a man in his favorite overstuffed chair. Even at that considerable height, Murray's posture suggested a relaxed and affable fellow.

I supposed nothing would go wrong on this second flight, but I supposed wrong. Moments later I heard Bobby shout, "Oh no!" and I whirled to see where he was looking, and that's when I noticed the small avocado tree down the hill to the right. It stood by itself, the only tree on that part of the hill, but the way Murray had the kite pointed, the tree was his natural target. A hush fell over the crowd.

Bobby yelled, "The tree, Murray! THE TREE!" and he started running.

This time, I thought, *Murray's had it.* Bobby's protégé was going to have the landing of his life, and I could hardly bear to look. His elbows were out and he was pulling back on the control bar like someone reining in a horse, and we heard him call out a distinct "Whoa!"

By then Lois and I and all the other flyers had started running. Lois screamed, "MURRAY! TURN THE KITE!"

Out ahead of us, Murray didn't. Or couldn't.

I thought, *Oh Lord, he's going to break his neck.*

Murray's second "Whoa!" did nothing to slow his galloping steed, but all that pulling on the control bar did insure a clean, straight dive right into the avocado tree.

For the second time that afternoon Murray Tanner disappeared.

Bobby covered the distance like a cheetah.

Trailing him by considerable yards, Lois and I jetted downhill until we came to a spot where we could see the kite clearly, perched atop a nest of branches. The odd thing was, we couldn't see Murray.

"Oh Lord!" cried Lois. "Where did he go?" She put her hand over her mouth.

But then the tree started to vibrate.

Bobby was already shinnying up the tree trunk, calling into the upper branches. "You okay, Murray? I'm coming up!"

Another tremor passed through the tree, and I glanced over at Lois. Her face was a little less tense.

"I hope he's all right," I said.

"I think he is." She was almost smiling now. "With the way he's got that tree shaking, I doubt there's anything wrong with him."

When Bobby returned to earth he had a bulletin: "Murray says he'll be down soon—as soon as he gets his pants loose from the branches."

We waited quite a while. And then Lois started to laugh and pointed at the tree and I could hardly believe what I saw: a pair of skinny legs emerged down through the branches, followed immediately by striped underwear.

"I'll go get your pants," Bobby offered, starting forward, but Murray told him not to bother, he'd shucked the pants because they were practically welded to the tree. "Forget it, Bobby. There's not enough left to put on."

All of which is why Bobby and I agreed, on the way home, that going flying was always an adventure, but if Murray Tanner was going to be there, the rest of us could hardly afford to stay home.

THE SPORT AND the business were so heady that year there were nights I could hardly sleep. While we were all on Maui, Bobby and Chris set an altitude drop record of 10,000 vertical feet, flying off Haleakala. Two days later, on Oahu, Bobby set a time-aloft record of 8 hours, 24 minutes, recorded in the *Guinness Book of Records.*

After we returned home from his honeymoon, Chris won the First U.S. Hang Gliding Championships and Bobby was runner-up. Coles Phinizy from *Sports Illustrated* came to the championships and featured Bobby and Chris in a long article in November, '73. Twentieth Century Fox invited Chris to come to Hollywood and consult on a major movie based on hang gliding.

It was all too good to be true. Superstitiously, I found myself looking over my shoulder—had I turned the stove off, removed the skateboard from the driveway, locked the back door? I kept hearing a small voice whispering in my ear: "When your cup runneth over, looketh out."

Chapter Twenty-One

Eric

THERE MUST BE some way of getting acquainted with a shadowy son besides going to work with him every day. If there was, I never discovered it. By the time Eric was 15, Glenn Johnson knew him better than I did—in fact Glenn's *mother* knew him better than I did.

In some ways he was like a bug living under a rock. You had to move the rock just to find him, and there he'd be with Glenn Johnson, having a rollicking good time, but not necessarily with us.

And then Chris came up with his breathless idea for a business, and suddenly the family *needed* Eric, needed him on a daily basis, and needed me, too, an all-purpose grown-up who could share an office with my cryptic son . . . and in the process learn what kind of kid he really was.

FROM THE DAY our business started, I grew close to Eric in ways that had never been possible in those earlier, hiding-out years. Now, because he and I were partners in paperwork and his desk was only a few feet from mine, I saw sides of him I'd rarely seen before. I was finally catching a glimpse of his inner spirit.

To be honest, I glimpsed his outer spirit, too. In spite of my protestations, Eric's hair had grown long again, down to his shoulders and wavy, and though my jaw tightened at the sight of my son looking like a disciple bound for Damascus, I had to swallow my antipathy and pretend those biblical tresses didn't matter. And finally they didn't. The truth was, I enjoyed working with him so much I nearly forgot the hair.

From the beginning I was reminded of his innate sense of thrift. Now, instead of clipping coupons for himself, he was trying to save money for us. "Why should we order two mops, Mom," he asked, "when we can buy a dozen for half the price?" And so he ordered three dozen mops—most of which Rob made us send back, knowing we'd be lucky to find anyone willing to mop the office even once.

Eric was alert, sharply attune to the young men who frequented our business. "Don't give that guy much time, Mom," he whispered as a lanky male customer drifted into the back. "He's never going to buy a kite."

"How do you know, Eric?"

"I've seen his type before. He just wants to hang out and ask questions. He's not a flyer, you can tell, he's just a curious guy who thinks this business is kind of crazy, not your normal people here. He thinks we're fun to watch, like monkeys. He won't buy anything."

He didn't. I wasn't quite sure how Eric knew.

When he wasn't guarding our manufacturing secrets, clamming up as customers' questions became more pointed, Eric was tracking down cheaper sources of supplies.

We were soon operating as a team, united against the world . . . and even against Rob on the one occasion when he lost touch with reality and turned irrational.

Early in our start-up days Rob came charging into the shop one day with what he assumed was an irresistible scheme: for a fixed amount, "a paltry sum," he called it, Wills Wing would offer Southern California ad agencies the chance to use hang gliders as billboards—meaning our boys would fly airborne advertisements a guaranteed twenty hours from all the hills around Southern California.

"They'll be like the Beetle Billboards," Rob said with his usual vigor, "you know, the ads on Volkswagen bugs."

Eric and I gave each other skeptical looks. Who would sign up for that? We assumed the idea would disappear like an ice cube, gradually melting away.

It didn't.

Instead, Rob created a clever letter and one day stormed into the office with stationery boxes full of them, plus boxes of envelopes. "Read this," he said, handing letters to Eric and me. He laid his boxes on Eric's desk. "Our kites attract so much attention we should have no trouble getting sponsors. Eric, I want you to send these letters to all the ad agencies in Orange and Los Angeles Counties."

I said, "Isn't nine hundred dollars asking too much, Rob?"

"Of course not. It's worth double that for the novelty alone."

Maybe, I thought.

Eric sat staring at Rob's boxes. "How many envelopes are there?"

Rob's tone became brisk. "A thousand."

"*A thousand!*" The number sent Eric right to his feet. "You want me to send out *a thousand letters?*"

"Yes," Rob said, "and don't be so afraid of a little work. It won't take long—a couple of days, at most. Just use the Yellow Pages."

Blocking further objections, Rob wheeled out the door.

Eric's generous mouth had become a thin line. "It *will* take long," he muttered, and pushed away Rob's letter with visible distaste. "I'll *never* be able to address a thousand envelopes. I couldn't finish *that* many in ten years."

I looked across at him sympathetically. "Maybe it won't be so bad. Just try. You can do it."

"Why don't *you* do it, Mom?"

Eventually he opened the phone book, worked intently for a

short while and stopped. When I left to go home, he was staring glumly into space.

The next morning I found Eric fingering the yellow pages without really doing anything. In front of him sat a tiny pile of completed envelopes addressed in his round, graceful hand.

"Come on, Eric," I said. "Dad wants this finished right away."

"Yeah?" he said. "Well he'll have to wait, 'cause the phone book is crammed with 'em. *Nobody* could do it. Not even you."

What could I do then but help?

That afternoon as I typed envelopes I made an unhappy discovery: the Carter Dunfiddle agency was also listed as Dunfiddle, Carter, and even a third time as The Carter Dunfiddle agency, and it was only because of the unforgettable Dunfiddle that I'd even noticed. How many duplicates had we already done?

As it turned out, a great many. "Oh boy, Eric, we're going to have to look up every name twice."

"That figures."

Chris happened by just then. "Don't look them up twice, Mom . . . Dad wants the mailing done, let Dad sweat the extra postage."

After two days of intense effort, Eric and I mailed a stack of 130 letters, leaving 870 to go, and I was growling, "This better pay off."

"Don't worry," said Eric. "It won't."

Another five days of work and Eric and I were blood-brothers united against the tyrannical Rob, who kept insisting the job was nothing and the two of us were just crybabies. But it wasn't all bad, because we'd finally figured out systems that cut our time somewhat. Then we purchased little gadgets, a letter-licker and a stamping machine, that cut our time even more, and we carried on with a certain pride (which we wouldn't have shared with Rob for anything), knowing we were probably the champion mail-out mailers in Orange County.

As pessimistic as we were about the outcome, we'd never have guessed the project would turn out quite the way it did. In the second week a scattering of letters came back marked, "Addressee Unknown," or, "Moved: Left No Forwarding Address."

At first they arrived in twos and threes, but after a while, with the mailing a third finished, they came back in quantity—some days, it seemed, faster than we were sending them out. Suddenly our volume of mail into the office had tripled, which seemed thrilling until we realized that most of it was our own letters winging their way back home.

After we'd sent five hundred without a single positive response, I said to Rob, "Why don't we wait now and see what happens? Five hundred's a pretty good sampling."

In one of his more unreasonable moments, Rob declared, "I want you to send them all! Every one! Even a two percent return will make it worthwhile."

If we got two percent, I thought acidly, *it would be a miracle right next to the loaves and fishes.*

I could see Rob backed into a corner, the man who never gives up pretending the corner was right where he wanted to be. I said, "You want this job to go from dumb to dumber, don't you?" and he said, "Just do it, you'll see."

We saw, all right.

That afternoon I told Chris, because I was too angry at Rob to say it to him, that I hoped we'd never need serious promoting, because ad agencies seemed to have the longevity of insects; they hatched, lived, and died during a single yellow pages season.

Another week went by and Eric and I finished the job, the best of buddies agreeing we never wanted to think about it again.

As it turned out, we didn't have to.

Except for our own letters returning like homing pigeons, we received only two responses. One was from a decent sort of man who took the trouble to explain that his customers would want a lot more for nine hundred dollars than we were prepared to give them, and the other, a penciled note on the top of our returned brochure: "Are you kidding?"

I COULDN'T HAVE felt closer to Eric. Soon after the mail-out fiasco, the two of us were like school kids poking fun at an unpopular teacher. "You see?" said Eric gleefully, fingering a pile of unopened letters. "I knew Dad was crazy."

"More stubborn than crazy," I said.

"He would never have done such a dumb thing himself. He would have quit if he'd been here to see it—all those letters flying back like boomerangs."

I nodded, because of course he was right.

"Next time I'm gonna tell him, 'If you want to be retarded, Dad, go ahead. Mom and I will watch.'"

WE HAD A great time, Eric and I—two worker bees in an office that hummed with activity. By the end of 1973, our world could not have been sweeter. Every day brought new excitement, not only championships and world records, but lesser events: Bobby and Chris made the sport's first tandem flight. Bobby, the Pied Piper of hang gliding, led foreigners and out-of-town pilots to all the new, exotic flying sites. Local newspapers breathlessly reported the boys' dramatic flying moments. Movie makers followed Bobby, Chris, and Ramsey Price to the hills.

Everything appeared to be going well.

Perhaps too well.

When Coles Phinizy summarized our family story in the November *Sports Illustrated*, he wrote, "In a sport so young and booming, the preeminence of the Wills brothers is apt to last about as long as the head on a glass of ginger ale."

I sat in the office reading his words with alarm. It was one thing for me to feel superstitious and another for him to forcast doom for all the world to read. He seemed to be presaging our ultimate downfall, and mentally I fought back. *You're wrong, Coles, we'll show you, we'll go on forever.*

Sadly, Coles Phinizy was right.

The next March Eric died in a hang glider accident.

Eric, 1973.

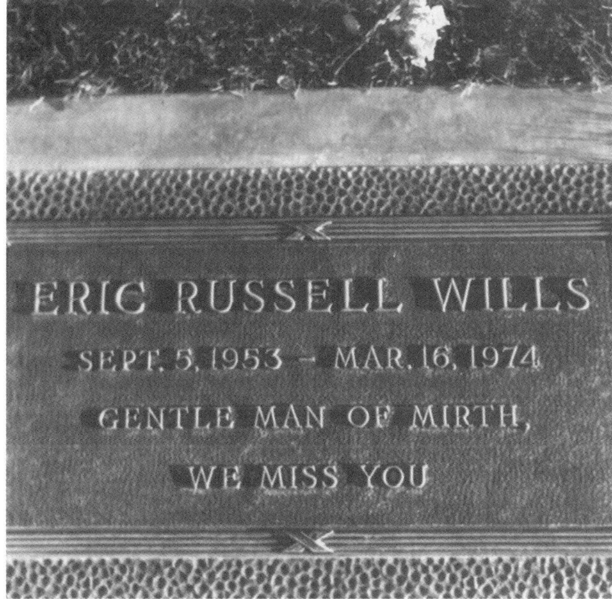
ERIC RUSSELL WILLS
SEPT. 5, 1953 – MAR. 16, 1974
GENTLE MAN OF MIRTH,
WE MISS YOU

CHAPTER TWENTY-TWO

The Rapture

ERIC. GONE.

This was not what I bargained for when I married Rob, this was not part of our deal. You aren't supposed to have all these kids and then lose one. *I didn't sign up for this.*

In our grief, Rob and I could only turn to the other children, and only with their help could we decide what to do next.

As a group, now only seven of the original family, we gathered in our living room, the one room we never used, to begin our sad discussion.

The scene was so unlike us: Bobby sitting on our fireplace hearth, head bowed, long legs extending halfway across the room. Rob staring into space because for once he had no words. The rest of us perched on formal, overstuffed chairs, unwilling to speak up because we all felt so terrible . . . and anyway, what was there to say?

Finally Rob asking, "What should we do with our business? You have to decide, Bobby. It's up to you."

A sudden cry from me. "Oh, no, Rob! That's not fair, we can't lay this on him. Either we keep the place open or we don't."

Chris asking, "Are you going to go on flying, Bobby?" All of us, even Chris, knowing this would not, ultimately, be Chris's life.

Bobby looking up with pain in his eyes, unable to say whether he would or he wouldn't.

And then at last, the rest of us making the decision for the one person who couldn't. Flying was most of what Bobby cared about. Flying gave him purpose—it set him apart.

Flying was Bobby's life.

In the end we were unable to take it away, so the next morning I went down to Wills Wing and hung an "Open" sign on the door.

SOMEHOW WE MANAGED without Eric.

For me, not very well.

Chris's best friend, Ramsey Price, tried to fill in as office manager, but when I came back to work and looked over at Eric's desk it was a shock to see Ram instead of Eric. For weeks, the good parts of life felt blasphemous: the first time I played tennis, the first time I laughed.

How can I play tennis knowing Eric is dead?

It seemed for a while as if our hang gliding business would never be the same.

Of course it would never be the same.

But our business and our family went on anyway—only different.

Ironic, I thought, as Rob was taking our annual picture in December. We still have eight people. Only this year one of them is not Eric. Instead, the eighth person is Betty-Jo.

WILLS WINGS, THE hydra which grew two heads every time we lopped one off, was incessantly consuming of our time and our thoughts, and gradually my inner dialogue changed and I realized a few hours had gone by when I wasn't thinking of Eric.

Yet I kept finding papers written in Eric's neat, rounded script and each one brought him back to me with a pang, and I felt the lump in my throat and the tears rising to my eyes. *Oh, God, I miss you, Eric.*

IN 1974 OUR business was laughably unprofitable. And now, without Eric to run interference, I had to cope with all the young hang gliding nuts myself . . . of which we seemed to attract an endless supply.

Take Jake, for instance. I'm not sure Eric ever dealt with him, but I do remember the first time Jake marched into our office . . . how he barked, "I'm going to be one of your dealers," and how, without the hint of a smile, he bought two hang gliders in a record twenty minutes. Chris offered him free flying lessons. "No time for lessons," he said as he charged out again, "Got a plane to catch."

He should have taken the lessons. Back in Minneapolis, he assembled a crowd at the top of a massive city landfill, set up the kite according to what he remembered from a brief demonstration in our shop, and ran off the edge.

I presume he expected to soar up, up, and out of there, into the Minnesota version of the Elysian fields. But having no clue about the principles of flight, Jake never got airborne, not even for a few feet. Instead, like a bird shot out of the sky, he and his glider plummeted into the dump below, dropping into old automobiles and wet garbage.

We never heard how he escaped from the dump with two broken legs, never learned who dragged him out, or how.

Once healed, Jake showed up in our office again, but strangely, his injuries had done nothing to temper his arrogance. With untamed bluster, he ordered more kites, and when he returned to Minnesota he ordered still more, and soon he was by far our biggest dealer.

But he drove us crazy. Me especially. He tormented me with irritating phone calls, always in a deep raspy voice that began, "Hello, Sweetie—this is Jake," or he barked to our new office manager, Roy, "It's Jake, here," as if Roy didn't already know, and his calls ended with Jake telling great whoppers about his orders and bullying Roy into putting *his* customers ahead of all others.

Roy knew Jake was constantly lying, but because we needed those Minnesota orders, Jake got away with blackmail. For two years he kept us afloat, though we disparaged him in tandem with his abuse of us.

And then he died. Tragically. Ironically. He died as he'd lived, in a kite-towing competition in which he broke every rule of the contest and brought about his own end. It's hard to report this even now, but Jake was sliced fatally by the towing cables as he tried to execute a maneuver everyone had told him not to do.

Even Roy himself had come to us as something of a character. A tall, gentle, soft-spoken man, he was a bit squirrely . . . and immune from being fired, since we never actually hired him. Like many people who became fixtures in our shop, Roy came out of nowhere. Thanks to a mysterious arrangement with Bobby, he just appeared in back one day and began repairing kites.

Soon we discovered Roy could do anything, from writing articles to keeping track of supplies and, with Ramsey Price back in school, he became the logical successor to Eric. Roy was much too thin, and Ram quickly discovered why . . . he rarely ate anything except Cokes and Twinkies, which Ram dubbed "Roy's vitamins."

Dougan Yeakel was another of our hang gliding characters. A friendly hanger-on, he was an ex-TV automobile huckster who appeared regularly in the shop, sneaking looks at our invoices and saying, "I can get that cheaper." Which of course he couldn't. One day, on a lark, he walked into the shop and shot real bullets through the target Bobby had painted on our ceiling. When I told him I didn't think that was funny, he climbed on the roof and repaired the holes, so that when it rained we got a trickle instead of a downpour.

Sometime during that year, religion swept through our shop like chickenpox, and soon all our workers, including Bobby, considered themselves "born again." The fellows in back converted one another, and I wondered how Eric would have reacted. Now, along with kite measurements written on the walls we found biblical passages. "For whosoever believeth in Him . . ."

By then my good friend Pat Ewald had joined me in the office, a tennis pal who was as intrigued as I by all the characters who frequented our business. Sometimes we two mothers thought we were the only sane people around. Still, we were fond of our youthful kooks, and between bouts of paperwork we listened patiently to sermons by a young worker named Peter, who began talking to us about the Rapture.

Curly-haired, blue-eyed Peter stood at Pat's desk and explained with a look of awe that one day Jesus would return to earth and sweep up all the good people in the twinkling of an eye. He added in a hushed voice, "Only the sinners will be left."

He made it sound quite threatening. But somehow I never saw myself as a sinner.

Then one afternoon Peter came out front and paused again in front of Pat's desk. "Do you know where John is?" he asked.

"No," Pat said, shaking her head.

Frowning, he glanced around nervously. "Where's Dave, then?" he asked, and I volunteered that he was probably out in the alley fixing a kite.

"He isn't there," said Peter, who was now turning pale. "And I can't find Mike, either."

Pat and I were beginning to get his drift: the Rapture. "Mike was here a short while ago," she offered. But somehow that didn't console Peter, who turned and threw a last despairing look around the office before disappearing in back. Clearly Peter felt doomed.

Pat turned to me with a rueful smile. "You know, Maralys," she said dryly, "he didn't seem the slightest bit surprised that *we* were still here!"

MY HOURS AT the shop became erratic, regularly giving way to such diversions as tennis and the frequent chauffeuring of our two youngest, Tracy and Kirk, to school and tennis tournaments.

I thought about writing another book, imagined myself doing it better this time and somehow getting published. Meanwhile, I wrote articles and made a few sales, though I also gathered more than my share of rejection slips.

In the year after Eric, I thought often about my remaining kids and how glad I was we'd had so many. It's not that one child could ever substitute for another . . . it's only that there were others left to love.

THE LAST OF them were growing up. Since Tracy was then fifteen and a half, and inevitably due for a driver's license, Rob began letting her drive us here and there on errands.

Tracy! I thought. *Driving!*

For some reason Rob managed to stay calm, even when she put our four-on-the-floor Capris sports car through a series of bumps and grinds worthy of a burlesque queen. As the three of us went slamming up Beverly Glen, jerking from one gear to another while the back of the seat gave us kidney punches and a whiplash, Rob calmly told Tracy to "ease up on the clutch . . . not that fast, not that fast . . . well, start the engine again."

I said, "If we don't get her out of the driver's seat, Rob, I'm staying home."

Then Tracy switched to an automatic transmission, with miraculous results, and at last even I stopped jamming my foot into the floor mat. Still, this didn't make her an expert, as we soon discovered.

One morning at six-thirty, while I was still asleep, she and Kirk went to the club for some early tennis. They decided to take the bucket of balls, but knowing they'd be scattering tennis balls like Johnny Appleseed if they tried to ride their bikes, Tracy boldly opted to take my car. After all, she *did* know how to drive, the distance was only half a mile, and presumably no one else was on the road.

As they explained later, all went well on the way up, but when they were ready to come home the car wouldn't start. Neither of them had the faintest idea what was wrong, but after a brief discussion Kirk decided, "It must be the oil; we'd better check it," which Tracy agreed was the next step. (What they thought they'd do about any imagined oil deficiency, one can only speculate.)

So far so good, except neither knew how to get the hood up.

Tracy began pushing levers and buttons inside the car, while Kirk probed with his fingers near the grill, and then Tracy got out to join Kirk at the hood, and after they'd both vented their frustration by kicking the car, somebody's finger accidentally found the latch and at last the hood let go and popped up.

After quite a bit of searching, Kirk located the dip-stick and drew it out and, as he told me gravely later, "There's hardly any oil in your car." He hadn't noticed the markings on the stick, he said, but he made it plain that an inch of oil on a two-foot stick had to be inadequate.

Having located (but not solved), the problem, they assumed they'd done enough, and now they had only to put back the dip-stick and drive home. But when Kirk started to push the rod back in, the thing wouldn't budge. Rob admitted later that the stick on that car had always been difficult, "like trying to thrust a bayonet into a bull," and Kirk realized if he tried to ram it home it might break off.

With the dip-stick poking up out of the engine, of course, the hood wouldn't close. The two were faced with a serious dilemma. It was nearly time for school, so Tracy quickly started the engine ("This time it started right up," she reported), and with the hood up and the dip stick pointing skyward and both of them putting their heads out the window to see, Tracy drove them home.

At times like that Rob and I found it hard to be proper, stern parents. Our record as disciplinarians was shakier than a Mickey Rooney marriage, because often, at the crucial moment, all we could do was laugh.

CHAPTER TWENTY-THREE

Bobby

TWENTIETH CENTURY FOX, the studio that had once summoned Chris repeatedly to Hollywood, suddenly stopped calling. We knew they were still making a major hang gliding movie, but their unspoken message was classic Hollywood: Don't call us, we'll call you.

As he'd done with other disappointments, Chris said almost nothing about the fact that he and Wills Wing had inexplicably been dropped. Around the office, he simply stopped talking about it, and concentrated instead on sending out applications to medical schools. "I've already mailed off twenty," he reported one day, "mostly because Betty-Jo is helping." He gave me a rueful smile. "I know this is costing Dad a fortune."

"Where better to put a fortune?" I said.

With a degree from UCLA but no medical school in the offing, Chris returned to work at Wills Wing. Here he was, back again, and instead of Eric helping from the next desk, it was Chris dashing through the shop, showering all of us with energy and high spirits.

"He's a real whirlwind," said Pat. "He's fun to have around."

"Isn't he?" I said. "But then he's always charmed me. He doesn't mean to, he just can't help it."

Yet for me, Chris's presence connoted a certain sadness. All of us knew this business would not be his life's work, that it couldn't be, in the long run. For Bobby, yes. For Chris, no. Five of us—Pat, Roy, Chris, Bobby, and I—all worked in the front office on a day-to-day basis, none of us certain what would happen next.

ONE DAY, WITHOUT warning, the boys' movie prospects changed again. Chris learned through the hang gliding grapevine that Hollywood stuntmen had been hired to make the Twentieth Century Fox movie. Almost at the same moment, Chris and Bobby were invited by the photographers, MacGillivray and Freeman (who'd filmed them informally in other settings), to join the stuntmen in producing a test film.

"Don't make waves," Greg MacGillivray warned Bobby. "You and Chris just come out and fly with them. And lie low. I can't make any promises about the movie itself. We'll see what happens."

With no real hope that this would do them any good, Bobby and Chris drove out one evening to a motel in the mountainous Palomar area, where they met Greg and some producers and the Hollywood stuntmen, who came with competing, but lower-performing kites. That night at dinner the head stuntman was patronizing. "I figure you guys have never flown for films before, so here are the rules. Here's what you do."

Bobby and Chris stared at their plates and did not protest that they'd actually done quite a lot of filming; they just listened and kept still. They went to bed that night trying not to feel cowed by the arrogance that had floated through the dining room.

But what happened out on the hills the next day changed everything. On the first day of filming it became obvious that the stuntmen had almost no hang gliding experience. "They can't do the simplest maneuvers," Chris reported back that night. "Some of them are such novices they won't go off the really big hills." I could almost see him grinning. His voice was tremulous with excitement.

By the end of that day, two of the stuntmen went home.

The next day's flying was harder, with added layers of sophistication. Bobby soared for a half hour above the face of the hill. The stuntmen virtually plummeted to the bottom—and one of them knocked over the cameraman. Before the second day was finished, their leader came up to Chris. "We're not up to this," he said. "I hate to admit it, but you guys are in a different league." He put out his hand. "Good luck, Chris, making the movie."

And so, in a kind of unintended fly-off, Chris and Bobby won back the movie everyone thought they'd lost.

The test film was spectacular. Rob and I went to the showing in Hollywood, where the studio big wigs saw the footage, now set to music, and gave it a standing ovation.

In the spring of '75, Chris and Betty-Jo and Bobby (and Bobby's new bride, Suzi), and four of their flying friends and a dozen newly-built Wills Wing hang gliders left by plane to make a movie in Greece. It was called *Skyriders,* and starred Richard Culp, James Coburn, and Susannah York.

Although Chris and Bobby and their friends did all the flying, their faces were never seen. But fame of a sort came to them later in a movie review that read, "Stuntmen Chris Wills and Bobby Wills flew away with the movie."

HOME AGAIN, CHRIS continued applying to medical schools. With his unspoken resolve in place he continued sending out applications. "Forty-two, now," he said grimly.

"How many more will you send?"

"As many as I have to."

In what seemed a miracle, New York University saved him the trouble.

FOR A YEAR and a half, Wills Wing belonged to Bobby and me (and peripherally to Rob.)

Chris and Betty-Jo were gone, living now in the heart of New York City. "It's all pretty different back here," Chris reported. "The cold. The formality. Living in a high-rise. At UCLA I never even wore shoes."

"You didn't, Chris?" I shook my head. One more thing I'd never known.

While the Wills Wing ship wasn't exactly sinking, Bobby and Pat and I were left to paddle and bail and try our best to keep it afloat.

But working with Bobby was nothing like partnering with Eric or Chris. During most of the hours I was in the shop, Bobby was somewhere else. Pat and I were always trying to find him, but he made it difficult. "The problem is," Pat said, "he operates in a different time zone."

"Did you ever think that you and I, two grown ladies, would be running a hang gliding company?"

"No," she said, "and I'm just glad it belongs to you and not me. I worry enough while I'm here. I'd hate to be fretting at home, too."

LIKE THE OWLS and the skunks, Bobby never did anything at normal hours—though I was still surprised the morning I reached him at home from Wills Wing, and right in the middle of explaining some vital business detail I paused, because he wasn't answering; instead I was hearing these strange, whispery nasal sounds, all very odd. And then I caught on. *Bobby was snoring! On the phone.* Even as we spoke, he'd fallen asleep and begun wheezing in my ear.

It wasn't funny, yet it was. Instead of shouting him awake I quietly hung up, because what else can you do when you're laughing? However many people I'd bored over the years, I'd never sent anyone into a deep, snoring sleep.

Similarly, Bobby thought nothing of stopping by our house at eleven-thirty at night, which he did one evening in June, 1977.

"It's nothing special," Bobby said as we opened the front door. "I just came by to say hello." And then he was striding into the family room, Goliath crossing Lilliput.

You take your grown kids when you can get them.

He headed for the kitchen, grabbed three cereal bowls, and passed around a box of Shredded Wheat.

Bobby was then twenty-six, married almost two years, with an eight-month-old son, Brandon.

Finished with his cereal, Bobby asked casually, "Did Kenny ever tell you about the time we got even with the Jensen guy next door?" He was smiling, and I could see it was going to be confession time in the old neighborhood.

"I'm not sure we've heard all your tales," said Rob.

I thought back to an earlier time, when George Jensen had been our next-door neighbor. A starched and humorless retired army colonel, he'd made it clear he had no tolerance for the slippage involved in a family with five boys. Thanks to the colonel's crabby disposition and frequent threats, the neighborhood boys had slyly demoted him, never referring to him as anything but Ensign Jenson.

We adults seldom saw the Jenson father, but that didn't hold true for our sons, who encountered him more than they liked, and always at the wrong end of a tongue lashing. The man seized every opportunity to bark at them like recruits, offering his dark opinion that they were hopeless hoodlums headed for reform school or worse.

Other neighborhood boys disliked him as fervently as our own kids, and even Jenson's sons were raised as second class citizens, forced to call their father "Sir," and forbidden to sit in, or even enter the family's white-carpeted living room.

Now, sitting across from us, Bobby grinned. "We got Ensign Jenson pretty good that day. He'd been shouting at us as usual . . . he thought he could say any old thing he wanted, and Kenny and I were sick of it. It happened to be a day Jenson was working out in his front yard, and I kept hoping we'd get lucky and he'd stay there awhile. Kenny and I had a plan, but we needed time."

Bobby laughed and sank down in his chair, extending his legs farther into the room. "Ken took the high bike and a walkie-talkie, and I went around the corner to the next street with my carbide canon and a sack full of oranges and another walkie-talkie.

"When I had my artillery loaded, I radioed Kenny. He'd agreed to be my spotter. So there was Kenny, talking on the walkie-talkie while he slowly rode the high bike down our street.

"I began shooting oranges out of the carbide cannon, aiming for Jenson's house. The first few landed on the roof and rolled into the backyard. I heard Kenny say, 'Higher and longer, Bobby,' so I made an adjustment. Then Kenny said, 'You overshot. The oranges are landing in the street. Shorten 'em up a tad.' That's when I opened up with a full salvo.

"I must have got it right, because Kenny hissed into the radio, 'Bulls-eye'!"

Rob and I were watching Bobby, mesmerized.

"Kenny told me later what happened. There was crabby old Jenson weeding out in his front yard, and suddenly oranges begin dropping all around him. He looks around and he looks up, and he barks, 'What the hell?' but he has no clue where they're coming from."

Bobby grinned. "Jenson can see Kenny riding along in plain sight, but he just can't figure out how to tie Kenny to all those oranges raining down in his yard. He keeps throwing suspicious looks at Kenny, but what can he say? Besides, Kenny is acting all innocent, riding and talking like nothing is happening. Finally an orange conks Ensign Jenson on the shoulder, and he says, 'God damn!' and throws down his weeding fork and goes inside. By then his front yard is swimming in oranges."

Rob said, "I'm glad we didn't know about this at the time." But he was smiling, and I, for one, wished only that I'd been out front to see it.

Bobby sank still farther into his chair. "There's probably a bunch of stuff you never knew about."

We talked for another hour, Bobby sharing stories of his old, battered truck driven for miles with stripped gears and no brakes, and how, when he passed an agricultural inspection station on the highway, he geared down as best he could, poked his head out the window, caught the inspector's eye, and yelled "No fruit!" as he sailed by.

He spoke of bedeviling the ushers of a drive-in movie by cavalierly riding his bike in the exit, until the young men, in desperation, got their own pint-size bikes and gave chase . . . which didn't do them any good, but did send Bobby into fits of laughter. "I could hardly ride, I was laughing so hard. You could hear those guys coming a mile away. Their bicycle chains squeaked, and they were pedaling with their knees up under their chins, and they looked completely stupid in their silly usher's caps. After that, there was no point in going back. It couldn't get any funnier."

We all fell silent, thinking of earlier times. He said, "Chris could probably tell you more stuff. If he ever gets home from medical school."

He stood and headed for the front door, then stopped. "I don't suppose you know that next week I'm going out to Escape Country to film a commercial for Willys Jeep."

We shook our heads.

"I'm filming with a helicopter." His expression darkened. "I made up my mind a long time ago I was never going to fly with a helicopter again. It's too dangerous. I decided the movie in Greece would be the last time."

"Then why are you doing it?" Rob asked.

He shrugged. "The pilot is George, the same guy who flew the helicopter for the movie. If it was anybody else, I wouldn't. But I trust George."

As he opened the door, *I thought, We aren't Bobby's parents any longer. We aren't responsible for him now. He can come to our house and tell us stories and we can relax and be amused.*

We were finally just good friends.

ON JUNE 24, 1977, Bobby was again out of the office.

"Do you happen to know where he is?" I asked Pat.

"Remember?" she said. "He's out at Escape Country, making that Willys Jeep commercial."

"Oh, right, he did tell us. He's gone so much I lose track."

I LEARNED LATER the assignment was finished when the filming helicopter went where it shouldn't have gone and left a cyclonic wake.

Because Bobby was faced the other way, flying through the back side of a turn, he never saw where the helicopter had been. As he flew unwittingly into the turbulence, his hang glider was seized as though by a giant fist and slammed into the ground.

An hour later, Bobby was dead.

Bobby's legacy still lives in the Smithsonian Institution's epic movie, "To Fly."

CHAPTER TWENTY-FOUR

Aftermath

BOBBY, THE SON who began our family, changed everything when he died. The wolf who'd been lurking in the shadows when we began the hang gliding had come once more to the front door; our hang gliding days were over.

When I learned Bobby was dead, I thought I would die too. Losing Eric was all I could take. The death of a second son was more than any mother could stand, and I was sure the pain would twist my heart and make it stop. I was seriously surprised that my heart went on beating.

For a while it seemed that 1977 brought our family an ending as sharp as a razor cut. Rob and I were beyond devastated.

But the sharpness eased a little when Chris came home from medical school and, like the oldest son he now was, took over for Rob and me. He investigated the accident. He gathered movies of Bobby to show at the memorial service. He organized the funeral.

I REMEMBER SO well the moments after the funeral. The crowd leaves the church and fills the social hall, and waits quietly while Chris works the projector. He makes a last adjustment. He says "Lights."

The social hall grows dim and I see an image flickering on a screen, an image that jumps and settles down.

Bobby.

Beside me I hear his wife, Suzi, draw in her breath, then she is quiet, we're both quiet, watching.

Bobby flies across the screen in front of us, turning abruptly to face us head on and wave, his butterfly kite with its red leading edges and large yellow circles on a blue field—beautiful, lyrical.

I feel better, suddenly. He is back where he should be. Here, in this setting, things are natural and right, the world is ordered again.

Bobby does a 360, turning easily, his pushing out thus on the control bar, his leaning against the turn bringing the kite full circle. He does it as though he were born knowing how.

My pain eases further.

Every scene is about him, as if he were summarizing his life for us in the way he might have done it best. Flying.

Suzi whispers, "It's so beautiful!"

In the dark I nod.

I think, *What does the number of a man's days matter if he's lived a lifetime?*

I remember his standing near the garage yelling at his father, "I don't want to do what everyone else has done! I want to be different!"

Well, he'd been different, all right. Wonderfully different. And he'd made the rest of us different too. And richer.

I watch him float away serenely, the sail rippling in a whisper of sound, the sun splashing across the fabric. One hand rests easily on the control bar, the other in his lap. Up here, I think, he is perfect. Flawless. This is Bobby, and this is the way he'll always be.

LATER, ROB'S PICTURES added another story. How could we have overlooked his pictures?

There they were, the two of them—Christy Wills (Chris's daughter), only eight months old when Bobby died, and Brandon Wills (Bobby's son), all of nine months. Only three weeks apart in age, the two were caught by Rob's camera sitting together on a couch . . . a couple of brand new cousins, clearly connected by age and background, yet nothing alike. Brandon was a sturdy little oak tree, while Christy was a delicate willow.

And so, as Rob and I began to recover from losing Bobby (and from losing Eric, too), and once more notice the world around us, it seemed that those two babies had moved seamlessly into our awareness. We could see that life and family, like a river, did indeed flow on.

Bobby's son and Chris's daughter remind us that life goes on.

Chapter Twenty-Five

Deep Sea Fishing

MOST MOTHERS WOULD have walked away from Wills Wing the day Bobby was killed and never come back. They would have slammed the doors behind them, as though locking up forever the memories that had now turned dark. I could understand such a reaction, I could grasp how some of us would burn to reject and punish a killer sport, that we would find in our hearts a bright hatred of what turned out to be deadly butterflies . . . the wings that pretended to be beautiful, while silently ready to kill.

I couldn't do that.

The sport was still Bobby's. He'd loved it and reveled in it. Like Chris, he wanted our business to succeed, but mostly because he felt passionate about our kites. Nothing pleased him more than hearing pilots rave about his hang gliders. For them, he would stay on the phone all day. I remembered his hanging on nearly an hour with a raver calling from Italy.

I went back to work with my chin set and teeth clenched. I'd lost Bobby and could never get him back. I was damned if I'd lose his business, too.

ROY WAS NO longer with us, so for most of a year Pat and I and a succession of managers and office managers (and then even Peter's mother, Marie), flailed about struggling to hold the business together.

With three mothers in the front office, Wills Wing lost its look of callow maleness. As it developed, mothers were sorely needed—especially Marie. By now Pat was doing all our bookkeeping, but flinching each month when she faced the task of sending in the payroll taxes. Often we didn't have the money. "At first I didn't know what to do," she said, "but I soon learned the solution was to tell Marie."

Quietly, and without making the front office look like a chapel, Marie prayed for the money. "One way or another," Pat said, "we always got enough—and always just in time."

Shortly before Bobby died, we'd hired three "kids" to help—and it was those three who eventually approached Rob, wanting to run the business.

Rob said, "I think I'll let them have it. I suspect they'll do just fine."

"But Rob, they're . . . kids!" I imagined they wouldn't do fine. I thought Rob's judgment was terrible.

Rob overruled me. In despair, I gave up and let him sell our business to three young people who couldn't possibly make a go of it.

But I was tired of struggling.

I wanted to go home and write.

MONTHS AFTER BOBBY was killed, while the mourning was still fresh in my heart, I could see those hang gliding years as a time set apart; they cried out to become a book.

I imagined such a book would be easy to write, that all I need do was sit down and fill pages and pages about a mother running a hang gliding business.

Believing that I was the focus, I began penning a mother's story, and in less than a year it was finished. My friend and agent, Pat Teal, sent it out.

Nobody came close to buying the book.

What could I do then but bind it and save it and find a new approach and start over?

PARTS OF OUR lives went on as they had before the tragedies. Rob still wanted to travel, he still yearned for family vacations, but the leadership among our children had shifted subtly. With Bobby and Eric gone, and Tracy nearly twenty, we unexpectedly found ourselves with a new family leader. Sometimes Chris was our moving force, but more often than not he yielded to Tracy.

Like Chris, she exuded enthusiasm. She poured energy into our family gatherings, bombarded us with plans, cajoled us into trying adventures we didn't care about. She made me shiver with excitement. In the end we always succumbed.

The deep-sea fishing trip was just one example.

EVER SINCE I read Hemingway's *The Old Man and the Sea,* I gathered that deep-sea fishing was a kind of sacred rite, not to be entered into lightly. And catching a "big one," like a tuna or marlin, was supposed to be the ultimate in "mystical experiences" . . . a transforming connection between human and proud, untamed fish.

Well, yes.

Unless your fishing expedition is led by someone like Tracy, who goes in and out of mystical experiences with breathtaking speed.

It happened more than once. At age 18 she talked Rob and the rest of the family into taking an exotic ski vacation in Keystone, Colorado, because, as she reported with her usual high excitement, "It's a fantastic, unspoiled resort, Dad. Dozens of different runs and you have them all to yourselves. I'm making reservations for everybody . . ." only to talk us all out of it again shortly after we'd arrived (before some of us even had our ski legs under us), when it appeared that Keystone was not quite as she'd envisioned—namely, it was extremely high and *very* cold.

"We've all got altitude sickness," Tracy declared on the third morning. "I've talked the airline into letting us come home early." And to everyone's amazement—and Chris's dismay, because he was actually enjoying himself—she had a party of eight whisked in and out of Keystone so fast we never really learned whether it was a fantastic resort or not . . . since most of those much-touted empty runs never saw a single pair of Wills skis.

While Tracy, at 19, was never similarly awed by the sea, she did declare to the family, then vacationing in Hawaii, "I've heard deep-sea fishing is something everyone should try—at least once." Her eyes were bright, her voice full of lovely excitement. Only a stone could fail to be moved. "Why don't we rent a boat tomorrow and go?"

By "we" renting a boat, Tracy naturally meant Rob, the father whose wallet she perpetually tapped, so engagingly, of course, that he seldom knew he'd been had. "Only" daughters are born knowing how to work their fathers—unlike sons, who have to learn.

Still, Rob had a few reservations, and while we were gathered in the condo living room, he expressed them to the entire group. "You realize, Tracy, that you and everyone else will be stuck on that boat whether you like it or not. And you may not like it—especially if you get seasick."

With her usual zip, zip, and away, Tracy shrugged off Rob's objections and went over his head to the rest of the family. "We *all* want to go—don't we?" And her lively gaze swept over Chris, me, Betty-Jo, Kirk, his friend Cathy, and Tracy's friend Greg.

A few nods here and there, and Tracy said, "You see, Dad? They all want to go." And to prove her point, she announced again, "We'll all chip in. We'll all help pay. Won't we?" and what could the group do but nod once more.

And what could Rob do but agree?

Having picked a charter boat with her usual dispatch, Tracy informed the captain with an air of authority, "Four hours won't be nearly enough. So sign us up for six, okay? We'll need six hours at least!"

It developed that the chosen boat didn't have room for all of us, so Betty-Jo and I volunteered to stay behind. We didn't mind at all. We'd been neutral about the whole thing anyway.

The next morning Tracy rousted everyone out of bed at dawn, having gotten up even earlier herself to make fishing-day sandwiches. The group left with a minimum of noise, while Betty-Jo and I went back to sleep, content with the thought that we'd have most of the day to ourselves.

I THOUGHT I was hearing things when, less than three hours later, I detected what seemed to be familiar voices coming up our condominium stairs.

It was them, all right, home from the seas, and five out of six looked decidedly peaked, and only Chris wanted to discuss the day in terms of fishing. The rest were fixated on how much they'd disliked being stuck on a boat.

Had there been a single experienced deep-sea fisherman among the group he would have known about the expected condition of the seas when the captain admitted over the phone the night before that recent fishing trips had been cancelled on account of "swells."

But to Tracy—to the entire family—the word "swells," with all its connotations of gentleness and cradle-like rhythms, did not sound threatening and certainly didn't deter them. "Twenty-foot waves," "crashing surf," "deep troughs"—those things our group would have understood.

Now the family flopped into chairs, and everyone except Chris began talking about the fishing trip as an adventure gone bad. They made faces and described the day in great, painful detail.

Only Chris had anything good to say.

It seems the swells began coming into the harbor before they'd even left the dock . . . big, heaving, voluptuous mounds, coming at them one after another. The boat hadn't reached the breakwater before it was bending from the waist, like an actor on stage, bowing first in one direction, then another.

Nor were the fishing lines even out when Tracy began to look around at the others and wonder desperately how she could tell them, twenty minutes into the trip, that she wanted to turn back.

Outside the harbor, the swells grew worse. The boat was now lifting and falling in the worst, the most un-rhythmic of patterns. Only Chris, sitting happily on a swivel chair at the back with a pole between his knees, and Kirk, leaning carelessly against the rail, seemed oblivious to the boat's bowel-churning motions.

A bare thirty minutes elapsed before Greg got sick—sick enough to crawl across the deck in search of a bucket.

Nearby, Rob was sitting on a deck chair feeling as if his insides would soon be outside. He happened to glance over at Greg, saw where Greg was heading, and shouted hoarsely, "Gimme that bucket!"

While Rob vomited into the bucket, Greg threw up on deck.

Cathy was lying on her back, trying to concentrate on whatever was not moving, like the sky . . .

That was when Tracy took charge. Struggling for balance, she lurched over to the youthful, bearded captain sitting at the wheel. "Can't you see we're all sick? Why don't you take us back?"

The captain stared at her without blinking. She had to be kidding. Hell, they were only minutes out of the harbor. You don't turn a boat around minutes out of the harbor unless there's some important reason, like a heart attack or a hurricane.

It was clear from his response he'd made an instant decision: ignore this ridiculous female and proceed with the trip. He gave her no argument, but he didn't turn back . . . and why should he? No such demands had come from anyone else.

The truth was, nobody else (except Chris and Kirk), was well enough to speak to him.

The boat dipped and tossed toward ever more mammoth seas, with the lines all out now, and the passengers mostly sprawled on deck.

At last Tracy pulled herself to her feet and marched on the captain again. "Nobody wants to stay out here!" she declared. "Turn back!" and finally he responded by turning the wheel. By now she'd made it clear that *she was in charge and this was her trip.*

They were scarcely into the return before the captain's mate shouted, "Fish on!"—an unnecessary cry—as Chris's pole was whirring with the sound of lines unreeling at enormous speed.

The two deck hands began dashing about excitedly. The captain turned off the engine and left the wheel, and the boat was now free to wallow in the ocean troughs.

The fish was a marlin—a beautiful, fighting creature, obviously huge. Chris, in sheer delight, felt the fish run with the line, saw it erupt out of the water twice and fall back again. Gripping the pole with both hands, he sat tight and responded to the instructions of the captain.

"We almost never get marlin this close in!" cried the captain. "You don't know how rare this is!"

For perhaps half an hour Chris fought the fish, while the deck hands hung over him, shouting advice and making preparations for landing the exquisite creature. All three had forgotten about the human cargo littering the deck.

To those sprawled up top, however, the time seemed endless. Greg had spotted the coastline and all he could think about was jumping off the craft and swimming away.

Rob was thinking they ought to get rid of the damned fish—on board or overboard—and get out of there.

It was Tracy who approached the captain again and said what the rest were thinking. "Can't you cut the lines and start the engine?"

"Cut the lines!" The man was incredulous. "On a *marlin?*"

"Anchovy or marlin, who cares!"

Now he *knew* she was crazy.

Turning his back on her, the captain shouted, "Get the bat!" and the mate brought something that looked to Chris like a baseball bat. The fish was near the boat now, rising to the surface, and the captain leaned over and in his intense excitement and eagerness to deliver a fatal blow to the fish's snout, he gave a mighty swing and the bat flew out of his hand and into the Pacific Ocean.

Apparently he wasn't the first to lose his weapon in a frenzied moment. "The other bat!" he bellowed, while the mate scrambled to fetch the back-up bat. This time the captain's aim was true and the fish was truly stunned by the blow.

By working fast and vigorously, the two boatmen and Chris soon had the marlin up over the side and deposited on deck. And now there were four humans and one mammoth fish sprawled on the surface, all in about the same general shape.

The boat got under way again and was shortly inside the breakwater, having reduced a six-hour trip to an hour and forty minutes.

As they docked, Rob growled, "Let's say good-bye to that stupid fish and get out of here."

"What do you mean, Dad," said Tracy, in the world's most sudden about face. "We're keeping it. It's our fish."

Even the captain was surprised. He gave her a look and said, "Of course I'll be glad to filet you a piece."

"Filet it!" cried Chris. "I was thinking stuff it—for my mantle."

Suddenly it was clear that no two people had the same agenda.

"Why would you do that?" asked Rob. "The rest of us never want to see that beast again."

"Yes we do," said Tracy. "We're taking it with us."

"*A hundred and forty pounds?*" cried Rob.

"It's his size that makes him impressive for stuffing," said Chris.

The captain broke in. "Nobody stuffs fish anymore. It's too expensive. I'll give you a nice chunk, though."

"What are you going to do with the rest of it?" asked Tracy.

"Sell it. For fifty cents a pound."

That got everyone's attention—even Rob's. Suddenly the thing had real, tangible value.

"But it's our fish," said Tracy again. "We paid for it."

Exasperated, the captain shook his head. "Unless you're running a seafood market or a chain of restaurants, you're going to end up with one big stinking fish on your hands." He had the marlin hanging by a hook now, and he pointed to it and smiled, trying gamely to bring back the conviviality of other, better trips. "Time for pictures!" he sang out.

Momentary silence. Since only Chris cared about the fish, in the end it was only Chris who spoke up and asked for a photo. And so Rob snapped his picture standing next to the marlin, one happy fisherman staking out an impressive prize. Judging by the photo, no one else was there.

Tracy was growing impatient. "Let's pay up and go," she said. And to the captain, "We were out less than two hours, so we'll pay you for four."

"Oh no!" said the captain, leaving the marlin abruptly to grab a notebook and a bill. "You signed up for six hours. So six hours it is."

At which everybody began protesting at once, all those eager fishermen who'd agreed to split the cost now morphed into a group of shameless skinflints, decrying the need to pay for a bunch of hours they hadn't used . . . until the captain threw up his hands in defeat.

Wallets came out all around, and when the money was handed over, the captain looked down in dismay. Four hours for the boat. Period.

Good sport that he was, the captain cut off chunks of marlin, more fish than three families could eat in a year, and was clearly glad to see everyone go.

Rob and I decided later that no wonder the two deck hands had been so excited when the marlin hooked up. From the morning's adventure they had expected to collect $210 for a six-hour boat trip, fifty cents a pound for most of the 140 pounds of fish, and a huge tip for delivering the ultimate prize.

Instead, what they got from our miserly bunch was the price for four hours of boat, most of a fish (but only because they fought for it), and no tip at all.

They'd seen better tourists. But hardly any that were worse.

THE MARLIN HUNG on like a disagreeable relative that refuses to leave. After that day we couldn't go out for a single meal. "We'll have marlin for dinner!" Chris cried that first evening. "This condo has everything, even a barbecue. I'll do the cooking." With enough tartar sauce, the fish was edible. Just.

"You girls can make marlin sandwiches," Rob said the next day. "They should taste just like tuna fish."

They didn't. And no amount of mayonnaise could save them from tasting like fish leather.

"You sure we want marlin again for dinner?" asked Betty-Jo the second night. "Isn't anyone getting tired of it?"

We were all tired of it. But somehow a fisherman's enthusiasm and a trip-leader's thrift won out over pleasure until, after the third night in a row, Rob finally said, "I'm through. I never want to see that fish anywhere near my plate again."

As we left to go home, Betty-Jo called her brother, stationed in Honolulu. "Meet us at the airport," she said. "We have something to give you," and she hardly dared admit what it was. As she thrust the last of our marlin into his hands, the rest of us stood around smirking and telling him how good it was, and how we'd eaten quite a lot, but the boat captain had given us this tad bit too much.

We were afraid to laugh, lest Betty-Jo's brother catch on and make us take it back. And then we'd have had to dump our precious cargo in the trash, which would have stunk up the airport and done serious damage to Rob's frugal psyche.

ONCE AGAIN, OUR daughter Tracy, with the enthusiasm and energy that has never known any bounds, had carried the day . . . make that several days.

But hey, I thought, *with Tracy leading the charge, events have a way of becoming memorable experiences—though not always mystical.*

Afterwards I couldn't help thinking about Bobby and Eric . . . that Bobby would have loved the ocean and the wildness, the "swells" of the sea, whereas Eric would have found a way not to be there at all.

The seasick landlubbers wanted Chris to cut the line, but he persevered.

CHAPTER TWENTY-SIX

Rummage

EVEN THE WORST tragedies don't seem to alter the basic personality of a real character.

Rob was something of a nut when I met him, and time has only magnified his eccentricities, some of which are endearing and others merely baffling. But the strangest of his eccentric traits started as a mere bud and blossomed into the biggest, damnedest, wildest flower any of us have ever seen.

I'm speaking of his yen to collect and save his possessions. Knowing Rob, I was astonished he had no interest in bringing home Chris's marlin. Hey, it would have made a spectacular statement over our mantle (but only after he removed the dozens of pictures and trophies already there). I can only assume the marlin reminded him of those long hours of being seasick, and nausea was not an event he wished to memorialize.

With other physical objects that pass through his hands, Rob assigns a value, and most he endeavors to keep.

IN 1978 ROB finally tackled a long-standing problem—our overloaded, bulging garage (which hadn't seen a car in decades). A few of Bobby's possessions needed storing, and perhaps he saw this extraordinary act as a memorial to Bobby. Whether that was true or not, I was just happy Rob finally viewed the garage as a problem.

Which brings up the mundane, all too earth-bound subject of rummage, about which I have a theory: Rummage is neither created nor destroyed; it is merely recycled among those who love it.

The fact is, half the world are rummage aficionados who, like Rob, throw up sandstorms of protest if their household partners try to throw away anything remotely useful. "Get that jelly jar out of the trash, Babe! It's perfect for storing nails." Never mind that he's already squirreled away—and so far isn't using—seventeen such jars—and more, if he only knew where they were.

The other half are the "tossers-out" who wait until the saver is dozing in front of the TV to bury the latest empty jelly jar deep in the discarded newspapers.

It's been my experience that every household has one of each, but by the time they mutually discover what they've married, it's too late. After all, Collector's Disease is never obvious at first; it's a latent malady that takes years to incubate. In the beginning, who has that much to save? But we tossers-out sense we're in trouble when we discover, early on, an old trunk that contains, among other things, our spouse's ninth grade essay on the Iroquois Indians, pictures of a fifth-grade girlfriend, a twelfth-grade math medal, and a tiny notebook half filled with high school vocabulary words, carefully tucked between two history textbooks circa 1939. If Rob and I ever moved—and I doubt our collection of hoarded goods would allow this—he would rather leave me behind than his precious childhood artifacts.

Even before I knew him well, I sensed I wasn't to be cavalier with Rob's "stuff." And then one day before we were married, I watched my future mother-in-law tuck her fingers into one of Rob's ratty shirts and rip it off his back. I was horrified. For a minute his expression veered between surprise and a threat of matricide. And then he finally laughed.

But that was her, I thought. It would never work for me. Still, I carried in memory the bright image of my mother-in-law's audacity.

Forty years later I got up the nerve to repeat her performance. Rob was walking toward me wearing an undershirt with holes so big a rat could have crawled through unimpeded. As he reached my chair I snagged the undershirt and ripped it off his body. The suspense was awful. Would he kill me or just break all my fingers? But sheer surprise blunted his annoyance, and all he said was, "Don't throw it away. It'll make a good rag."

Like all gifted rummage devotees, Rob has the uncanny ability to keep rummage circulating indefinitely. While he is happy enough to give to his children, his grandchildren, and friends whatever they might want out of our garage (unfortunately, nobody wants much), only in the last few years has he stopped purchasing nifty wooden furniture (like a big oaken coffee table we can't use), at the Salvation Army thrift store. But that's only because he knows he'd have to store the thing in some weird place, like under his bathroom sink, because the garage is now crammed from wall to wall and up to the rafters.

Knowing all too well he had a space problem, and in spite of encroaching jelly jars, wicker baskets, aluminum tubing from our hang gliding days, ancient steamer trunks, tables made from sliding closet doors, cans of crusted paint, and empty drawers from cabinets that no longer exist, Rob managed for years to maintain a trail out in his garage—up one side, across the back, and down the other.

But recently parts of the trail have become overgrown, until the garage is now so blocked there are areas I haven't seen since the early nineties.

OVER THE YEARS Rob has gathered treasures from a lot of peculiar places, including from along the freeways . . . which I learned about years ago as we were driving down I-5 and he suddenly swerved to the right and bumped off onto the shoulder, with a precipitousness that made me think he must be having a heart attack. "What are you doing, Rob? What's wrong?"

Jerking the car to a stop, he leaped out without answering. When he returned, he was hauling a large wooden pallet, which he forced into the trunk, turning and tipping it until somehow it fit.

"What's it for?" I asked, bewildered.

"Pallets are great for stacking firewood," he said. "I wish I had a dozen more."

Eventually he did have a dozen more—all discards, all scooped up with that look peculiar to a Natural Collector, a look I could only call poorly-suppressed glee. From time to time he also stopped to pick up jackets, hats, garden tools, wastebaskets, sweaters, carpenter's tools, and gloves.

Once on a ski trip he found a matched pair of orange ski gloves—one on the way up the mountain in the morning ("What do you want with one glove, Rob?" I asked with all the sarcasm I could muster, "You need it for your one hand?"), and the other miles away and hours later on the way down. It was the ultimate rummage-lover's triumph; he's never stopped talking about it.

After a while our kids, in their early teens, caught on to his tricks. He'd walk into the family room dangling from his fingertips a not-quite-perfect piece of clothing. "Look, Eric, a great new jacket."

"New?" Eric asked.

"New to you. Try it on."

Eric took the jacket gingerly and held it away from his body. He had already guessed the truth. "You got it off the freeway! Didn't you, Dad? The freeway!"

"Well . . ."

"I don't want clothes off the freeway."

"It's a perfectly good jacket."

"Ugh," said Eric, who always seemed to get the gifts from strange places—like the Christmas sword from Kenny's bedroom. He let the jacket fall as though it was nasty, as though his dad had handed him a horse turd.

Still, Rob couldn't quit. "Freeway shopping" proved as irresistible to him as gambling . . . as addicting as street drugs . . . until the day he happened to be following a diaper service van onto a freeway off-ramp. The van took the turn too fast and its back door flew open and a great white sack flew out onto the shoulder.

The van never slowed, but Rob did. With his usual great reflexes, he brought his car to a fast halt near the fallen sack. *Rags!* he thought. *Dozens of perfect rags.*

Exulting in his prize as only Rob could do, he grabbed up the bulging pouch. But a surprise was waiting. The sack was sure enough full of diapers. But the diapers were dirty!

Any other man would have blown out his breath in disgust, dropped the sack like a hot coal, and backed away with his stomach churning.

Even Rob was perplexed for at least one whole minute, knowing he was contemplating a treasure, which if brought home, might be grounds for divorce. He solved his dilemma by taking his smelly load to the nearest Laundromat and putting it through twice.

I've never let him forget it. "Six kids, Rob, and you never washed a single diaper, not once, not ever, but you were willing to wash that disgusting load off the freeway. What is there about a sack falling off a truck that melts your heart?"

"I guess the fact that it's . . . free."

ROB'S BEHAVIOR IN 1978 proves that the rummage disease is progressive. That was the summer Rob decided to "take the plunge" and reorganize his beloved garage. Having made up his mind that the contents must be sorted, categorized, and re-stored neatly (no mention of "disposing," no thoughts of "tossing out"), he enlisted Kirk and me and Tracy and her friend, Greg, and a young male English house guest to transport everything from the interior out to the cemented area known as "the blacktop." The Englishman was stuck. As a guest, what could he do but act enthusiastic and pretend he really wanted to pitch in and help the host family eradicate its all-too-obvious disease? He didn't know, of course, that the malady was incurable.

With all of us working diligently, it took three hours just to move the stuff thirty feet.

We could hardly get out the back door, now, and the junk was a blight on our backyard, but still it was a relief to see Rob and the English youth starting to reorganize the tools. All Labor Day weekend they labored and then, three days later, just as the gang of us were sitting in the station wagon ready to head for Las Vegas and a suite at the MGM Grand, someone turned on the car radio and heard that *rain* was forecast! Here! In September!

In disbelief, because Southern California never gets rain in early fall, we all jumped out of the car and threw everything back in the garage—tables, bureaus, couches, books . . .

The garage was now a worse mess than before. Back home a week later, Rob called us together once more to move out the stuff. His crew—even the Englishman—was noticeably less enthusiastic than they'd been on the first go-around, but back we came and out it went. Our mess was once again on display to whoever might have the nerve to use the back door.

Another session of poking through stuff.

And lo! A few weeks later, after the Englishman had departed, Rob wanted his goods returned to the garage once more because we were leaving for Europe and a second unseasonal storm was brewing.

"For Pete's sake, Rob," I cried, "just cover your stuff with a tarpaulin!" This was getting ridiculous. The contents of our garage had moved more times than we had.

But he only agreed to cover part of it, and as for the rest, his family reluctantly shouldered the tables, the lamps, the chairs, the books, back into that spooky, webby cavern known as the Wills Garage.

Once home again, out came our peripatetic rummage.

I began noticing that whenever a close friend or relative came by, he always cast an eye over our blacktop and he always asked Rob, "Can I help you move some of this stuff?"

I've often said I could see no answer to our garage problem short of the garage burning down. Secretly, I've longed for selective arson. But that solution became useless with everything out on the blacktop. There finally came a day when I decided if the garage did catch fire, I'd be out there myself, hurling the stuff into the flames.

NOW, TWENTY-THREE years later, Rob has added nine file cabinets to the mix and, with the cabinets full and blocking all access to the interior, the place has become so impacted only dynamite could break it loose.

The Wills family garage has finally become one of the Seven Wonders of Rummage—which our grown kids are fond of pointing out whenever they and any of our friends—or theirs—happen to be in our house at the same time. "Come see Dad's garage," Chris said recently to our close, longtime friend, Patty.

Together they went out to take a look, and Patty gasped in amazement and then laughed so hard she had asthma for an hour.

CHAPTER TWENTY-SEVEN

Family Feud

WITH A FAMILY that's broken, you heal when you heal. After awhile Rob and I seldom spoke about Eric or Bobby; discussing them aloud would have brought us unnecessary sadness, like poring over their possessions or recounting their deaths. Rob didn't want more reminders than he already carried in his head.

As for me, I lived with Bobby and Eric almost daily—but I recalled mostly the earlier, brighter years, the happier times that I was spinning into words, crafting scenes for *Higher Than Eagles,* my story about our years in hang gliding.

MEANWHILE, ROB PUSHED ahead with our activities as they'd been before our family changed: the trips; the family pictures; the pursuit of ideas; the sending kids to college; the evenings at the theater. In a way we'd closed ranks.

Still, he listened when one of our children proposed something new. Sometimes he was skeptical; but he listened.

It was Tracy, as it was so often now, who came up with the idea that propelled the family into yet another adventure. "We should all go on Family Feud," she announced one day with her usual verve, with that electrical hum of excitement that so animated her voice. As always, her enthusiasm was contagious. "My best friend's cousins tried out for the show, and you can earn lots of money."

I wracked my brain for a connection. "What's Family Feud?" I asked.

"Never heard of it," said Rob.

Undismayed by our ignorance, Tracy explained that this probable fountain of money was a TV game show that would fit our talents perfectly. She didn't need to add that the Wills family is nothing if not competitive, and while our members might not schuss down ski slopes tossing a football back and forth, they've been known to do other stupidly competitive things, like fly hang gliders while hanging by their knees. Beyond that, they're always contentious.

"I've got their phone number," said Tracy. "I'm going to call them."

"Sure, sure," said Rob, clearly not expecting anything to come of it. "Go ahead and try your magic."

Since of course I'd never watched the show whose name I didn't recognize, Tracy's idea had all the reality of a family debut at the Met. "Okay with me," I seconded.

It wasn't until Tracy produced an actual date for our interview that her plan acquired substance. "Which of us are going to do it, anyway?" Rob asked. By then we knew the show required five people, all related by birth or marriage. We also knew that one of them wouldn't be Chris, who was still back in New York, immersed in medical school.

Tracy said she thought the three of us, plus Kenny and Kirk.

"You'd better ask the other two. Make sure they're willing."

Tracy is nothing if not quick off the starting block, and within the day she'd secured Kenny's grudging agreement to participate if it didn't interfere with classes (he was then in Pepperdine Law School), and his even more grudging consent to watch the show at least once. She had also taken a reading on Kirk, which was that he was somewhat interested, had never seen the show, would probably never see the show, and might appear if given enough reminders—if we could even find him to remind him.

About then Tracy and Rob and I figured we had four-and-a-half contestants, and one of them a shaky half at best.

"Who else is there?" Tracy asked, worrying aloud. And abruptly she answered her own question. "Suzi . . . Suzette!"

An excellent choice, we agreed. Of all the family members then in California, Bobby's widow Suzette was the ultimate parlor games competitor. She habitually brought her favorite board games to our house, taught us the rules, then beat us. Besides, with her photogenic features and attractive blonde hair, she'd give us an edge in front of the cameras. Tracy quickly got on the phone.

She came back smiling: Suzi was willing.

In a mood of high excitement, four of us left for Hollywood on a Wednesday night, but not before we'd arranged with Kenny to drive from Malibu and meet us there—and found to our relief that he had watched the show—once.

The producers had warned Tracy we'd better 'dress up,' and we were dressed—fit to kill. Ties, stockings, heels, the lot.

Our first interview was held at what seemed to be a deserted Crocker Bank building on Sunset Boulevard.

We rode to the 14th floor and found the elevator doors opening to a full view of Kenny, sitting right there wearing a sleazy leather jacket.

"You'll have to get rid of that jacket," Rob whispered immediately.

Kenny bristled. "What's wrong with my jacket?"

"It's, uh . . . like plastic," I said. "It looks cheap," which merely inspired our son to draw himself up stiffly and pull the jacket in close. Rob and I shrugged. Maybe they liked shiny leather jackets.

In a small room crammed with families, we signed in, filled out cards, had our group picture taken. We studied our fellow competitors. The room was jammed, and from adjoining rooms came sounds of noisy try-outs—and clearly they were all practicing Family Feud enthusiasm. Such outbursts of cheering and clapping, obviously contrived, produced frowns on the faces of Rob and Kenny, who looked as if they'd just caught a whiff of overripe gym socks.

"You hear that?" said Tracy, "we have to be enthusiastic!"

Kenny responded by rolling his eyes heavenward, and Rob growled, "I have no intention of appearing ridiculous."

"Never mind," I offered quickly, "Tracy and Suzette and I will do it for you." I was fairly sure Family Feud wouldn't be interested in a family who was already feuding—in the waiting room.

Our turn came and we tried out. Nervously. An obviously sharp young stand-in named Phil ran us through a mock game with another family, and as many times as Tracy and Suzette and I had cautioned each other and the dead-serious guys to 'act enthusiastic,' even we forgot and focused instead on the questions. Every once in a while one of us remembered to clap or cheer, which sort of fired up the others momentarily. Or Phil would remind us: "Hey, don't you *care* that he gave the right answer?" and we'd do it again—burst into brief spasms of false jubilation until, like spent fireworks, we fizzled out again.

We won our three rounds and managed to smile a lot, but we weren't the "cheeringest" group they had.

Even afterwards when we told ourselves, "Getting the right answers meant nothing, you know, it's how we *behaved* that counts," we fell back into discussing the questions: "What's another food that people order on dates?"

Having been told in advance that any given family had only a one-in-sixty chance of making the show and we'd hear or not hear within two weeks, it was more than exciting when Phil called the next day and told Tracy, "Well, you've made it past me."

Another date in Hollywood, this time to see the producer, Howard Felsher. While we waited, once again, for our formal interview, Phil told us we could play a couple of practice rounds with another family. "Jill, here, will be your host," he said, pointing to a smiling brunette. I assumed she was an assistant producer.

Jill could not have guessed what was coming.

She led us through two questions against a family of cheaters—four lawyers and a mother whom we'd seen sneaking looks at the producer's cue cards. Naturally, they came up with every correct answer . . . which might have been merely annoying, except that Kenny took the cheating as a personal affront and began muttering and growling, as though someone was snatching his bone. As much as the rest of us yearned to throw a dog-catcher's net over him and haul him out of the room, we couldn't stop his pointing finger or his accusatory comments. The other family was embarrassed, Jill was startled, and I imagined we were dead. Our attack dog had done us in.

About then Phil appeared and called us for our "real" interview. To my surprise, Jill re-joined another family, and I realized we'd been saved. She wasn't a producer after all, she was one of us.

Waiting in the hall to be ushered into the presence of the all-important Howard Felsher, we adjusted our clothing and our faces, and Tracy and I whispered, "Remember, smile—be enthusiastic," and Rob said through clenched teeth, "If anyone tells me to smile again . . . !" just as Phil waved us toward the tryout room. Like shameless hypocrites, everyone, including Rob and Kenny, donned big, false smiles and marched toward the open door.

People-wise, Howard Felsher was a genius. He spotted everything. He interviewed us all in depth, and when I said I'd won a few club tennis tournaments, he noticed Rob's expression and asked, "What are you smiling about, Rob?" and Rob said he thought tennis was the least of my accomplishments.

He asked us about the family's involvement in hang gliding, declared we were all crazy, asked Tracy if that blond boy in the audience was her boyfriend and would she marry him if he proposed (Tracy blushed and fumbled out, "Well . . . not now"). He also asked Rob if he'd defend even obviously guilty doctors, and if so why. Rob said, "Because they need defending most."

He led us through several game questions, and Kenny, with the ultimate in courtly demeanor, trotted out the gracious manners he'd misplaced an hour earlier. I thought, *Well, here's a kid who figures out when to behave.*

Once again we were told we'd hear in two weeks.

Once again we heard in three days, and soon we had a taping date.

The written rules were explicit: show up on time or you're out.

Wear the right clothes (nothing white) or you're out. Bring two outfits apiece and no more than ten guests.

For once we allowed ourselves plenty of time to get to Hollywood, and thank God we did. At the last minute Suzi was stuck without a car, and it took a mighty, breathless scramble to get us all assembled in one vehicle.

Miraculously, we still had the hour we needed to get to Hollywood.

Once at the studio, we were shown to a dressing room with our family name on the door . . . and there sat Kenny. He looked great. Real cloth suit, smart tie, pleasant expression.

We had our own sink, mirror, closet, coat hangers—and TV! Up and down the hall were other rooms with other families whose names were on the doors. Seven families in all, and they'd be taping five shows.

After filling in numerous forms, we were led to the studio, where no fewer than four people took us through an hour of warm-ups. After a couple of spirited girls conducted family introductions, we all practiced 'enthusiasm,' and before long we were shouting answers in chorus—even Kenny and Rob. Third among our mentors was the wry director who suggested that in case we lost we were not to "slink away like dogs."

Fourth warmer-upper was Howard Felsher himself. He gave us the rules in tones of, "I'm not kidding and you'd better take me seriously." Any infraction, he said, and we could still be sent home and a stand-by family called in. We would not cheat or even look like we were cheating; secret monitors were in the audience watching us one-on-one. We would speak loudly. We would look and act enthusiastic.

Felsher made it sound like one frown and you're gone.

My face was slowly freezing solid in the happiness mode; I'd never felt so much pressure to look bright-eyed and giddy.

Warm-ups over, the studio served us a buffet supper and, like ants, we carried it back to our dressing room, which was beginning to feel like our own little ant hill . . . and the only place where we dared stop smiling.

Afterwards we all changed into party clothes and turned on our closed-circuit TV and sat there watching the first of our small band of families appear under the great, bright lights.

Two tapings later they called for the Wills family.

The show itself? Richard Dawson's kisses were playful, a lot more innocent than I'd imagined. And he was nicer and funnier than I'd imagined. But for us the show was over in a flash. We almost won it, we could have won it, we should have won it, but we were up against incredible opponents. We had slow hands, which wasn't so terrible, except the McKinnon family managed to give the number one answer to five different questions—*five times in a row*—which meant their family got to play every round, and all the Wills ever did was huddle off to one side and try to steal the round back—which the show calls "caucusing."

Even then, we won two rounds by caucusing and were ahead at the last question. On that last question, Suzi, the first of our crowd to do it, got her hand up faster than her opponent, gave the number two answer, but was downed when the brilliant "McKinnon" mother gave the number one answer, and the McKinnons had only one slot left to fill.

They missed twice, and it was like the bases loaded, three balls and two strikes, because our group knew the right answer. We decided later we might have mouthed the key word a bit too audibly as we were whispering among ourselves—loud enough so their player heard it.

At any rate, their third man gave *our word.*

So the McKinnons won and the Wills retired—and of course we went slinking away like dogs. Our net reward was $296.00 to divide up, plus some consolation gifts—costume jewelry and Mary Kaye cosmetics for the gals, and a meat slicer and wallets for the guys. And a bunch of mixed emotions . . .

WE THOUGHT THAT was the end of us and Family Feud, but it wasn't. Nine months later Phil called to ask if we'd like to be on the show again, and we jumped at the chance.

The second time we had none of the traumas of our first

appearance. We all did reasonably well, but Suzi was our star. On each of her turns she came up with the perfect answer, and this time, thanks largely to her, we bested the other team and made it to the fast money.

It was too bad we didn't choose Suzi to play the final portion as well, but we didn't. We assigned it to Tracy and Rob.

Tracy went first and gave enough high point responses to give Rob a shot at winning. Rob, too, eked out mostly good answers. But then he did the unthinkable. Richard Dawson asked him, "Name an animal with a beautiful coat," and after a long hesitation Rob said, "camel." He made a face and so did Dawson—a quick look of surprise. Rob went on, but he'd done us all in. "Camel" garnered no points at all, so we lost the big prize—the ten thousand dollars.

Afterwards, Dawson was openly laughing. "How did you happen to come up with *camel*?'"

"Well," said Rob, "I quickly went through a bunch of animals, like 'vicuna,' which I knew wouldn't be there, and the pressure built, and then a camel coat flicked through my brain and . . . well, you know the rest."

"That's got to be one of the funniest answers I've ever heard."

"I'm glad it was good for something."

FOR MONTHS AFTERWARDS people stopped Rob wherever he went to kid him about his camel, and people gave us little camels as reminders.

A year later, it was Suzi who put things in perspective. She said, "The ten thousand dollars would be gone by now. But camels are forever."

Rob's "camel" cost us $10,000.

CHAPTER TWENTY-EIGHT

Stomping at the Savoy—by Ken Wills

WITH ALL THE stories I wrote over the years, not many concerned our fourth son, Kenny. I'm not sure why . . . unless it's because he was overshadowed by the offbeat lifestyle of Bobby, the breathless aeronautical exploits of Chris, and the bad-boy shenanigans of Eric.

I realize now it's possible for a strong personality to be submerged in a large, growing family—for years!

Kenny, who in his early years was noteworthy as a spelling champ and a doggedly-committed swimmer (a swimmer-with-a-future), metamorphosed, after he arrived at UCLA, into an adventurer and bon vivant. Perhaps it took leaving home for a "normal" son like Kenny to emerge from the shadows and entertain himself by creating an offbeat persona of his own.

Certainly I never knew until he was grown that Kenny had always loved and admired his older brother, Eric; that it was Eric he thought about and Eric whose mischievous spirit he'd wanted to emulate. It just took Kenny a while to get around to it.

One would think that being off the mark or even displaying chutzpah was a requirement in the Wills family.

It wasn't. So don't ask me how this kept happening. I honestly don't know.

NOBODY COULD HAVE been happier than Rob and I that Kenny was able to spend some time in London. We'd always loved the British Isles ourselves and hoped our kids would grow to enjoy them, too. But so far, only Kenny has really experienced England in any depth.

And only Kenny can adequately describe what he did there. This is his story:

In October, 1981, I was in London, nearing the middle of a semester abroad in my final year at Pepperdine Law School. I was living at the Cromwell Hotel, a tired old place in South Kensington that was more hostel than hotel. By day we students attended courses taught by barristers and solicitors, and by night were free to do the things that poor but adventurous American students traditionally do in large European cities.

One Saturday night, I asked Colleen, a young blonde Irish desk clerk at our hotel, to come with me on a long walk to Dirty Dick's, in the East End of London. The place has a sawdust floor, good warm ale, filthy patrons and, on the whole, an atmosphere delicate people would find repugnant. It also sports ancient, desiccated (and very dead), cats and rats that were nailed to the ceiling beams centuries ago; the beams and their dusty companions are just inches overhead. All in all it was exactly where I wanted to start the night.

One never quite gets away from these rats and cats, and in the late evening the drinkers at Dirty Dick's often toast their memory and lament their suffering. Oddly, Colleen didn't want to spend an entire evening in this maudlin setting, and asked if we could leave for supper at a more conventional pub.

On the way back, walking near the Thames, I caught sight of the Savoy Hotel. I knew the name but little else about it. From the outside it was grand and opulent and had many well-dressed footmen, doormen, coachmen, bellmen, yeomen and gentlemen's gentlemen milling about its entrance. Black taxis chugged to the roundabout, disgorging ladies in long satin gowns and men in tuxedos. "Lovely," murmured Colleen. "Fancy us going in there."

I thought for a few seconds.

"Why not?" I said. "Let's see if we can get past the front door. I'd like to see the inside."

"Oh, Ken, we can't do that," she said. "We aren't dressed properly."

"We're here. Follow me."

She giggled. "Are you sure?"

"Of course."

I was wearing jeans and a baggy sweater, and Colleen was in a plain blue cotton dress.

Like a school of fish, the Savoy employees were in constant movement in and out of the front doors. We needed to enter at high tide and pour through as though we were on a mission. I explained to Colleen the basics: a brisk walk and forward gaze, and not the slightest degree of self-consciousness. I hoped she would also—somehow—be able to display a variant of my well-practiced look of irritation, or even menace . . . if she did happen to make eye contact with any persons legitimately on the premises.

We walked rapidly and purposefully up the steps to the door.

The Savoy's equivalent of the Beefeaters saw us coming and they did not hurry to open the doors. I frowned, spoke a few sharp but unintelligible words, and blew on past. Colleen slid in behind me. Our momentum propelled us through the lobby and, avoiding at all costs any face-to-face with potential ejectors, we headed down the stairs to the floor below. Downstairs, I began opening doors and peering into large, empty public rooms.

Then I opened a set of doors and stopped. This was the ballroom—as magnificent as any I'd seen. In this vast palace of a place, hundreds of formally-attired people were at dinner. Chandeliers glowed, candles flickered, and the tinkling of crystal and china met our ears. Colleen and I stood a moment and stared; I closed the door and we backed away. Just outside was an unguarded table, and on the table sat a small rectangular box that contained several unclaimed envelopes. Naturally I took one, and quickly led Colleen into a quiet room, where the two of us could read it without being noticed.

The invitation inside explained everything. The event was a patron-of-the-arts dinner following an earlier music performance at Royal Albert Hall. The tickets must have cost a grand.

Right then I decided the event needed two more patrons. Us.

I was considering how to handle the situation when a woman entered, and we realized we were in the ladies' parlour—fine for Colleen, but obviously not for me. We fled the room, but somehow left the outer envelope, which contained the names of the guests we intended to become. With the other lady still in the powder room, Colleen did not want to go back.

It was obvious to me that we were destined to attend the dinner, though by any rational analysis this presented quite a logistical challenge. Everything was wrong—our ages, our attire, our accents, and, most of all, our absence from the guest list. Our appearance alone was nearly insurmountable. I doubted there was a single man wearing jeans and a sweater in the entire hotel, let alone in the grand ballroom. Once inside we would be in the company of tuxedoed men and bejeweled women. Nobody, anywhere, was wearing a house dress.

Oh, what the hell, I thought, and led her back through the doors. With an affected air of haughtiness and indignation, I stood in the doorway, holding my invitation, as I signaled a nearby employee. To the hostess who quickly approached, I said, "I've just arrived from the United States. My plane was late. I've already missed the concert and half the dinner. We've had no time to change. Please seat us immediately." I made it up as I went.

She looked at us and paused. Her hair was pulled back in a severe bun and her posture was as stiff as the hair. And now, so was her expression. She appeared not to believe me. "Sir, what is your name?"

For just a moment I said nothing. Having lost this crucial bit of information, I grabbed another name quickly. My own.

As Miss Hairbun referred to her list, I suspected this would be the moment we'd be bounced from the Savoy. We were now inside the ballroom and in full view of all the guests. If we were ejected, a lot of fine and dignified people would be forced to witness the degrading spectacle. I pointedly looked at my watch—employing exaggerated head and arm movements. As she searched the list, I added a few critical remarks about the inept airline and our lamentable state of decline, pointing out that we were exhausted and hungry and put out and would appreciate being seated without further delay.

I recall the occasions when my mother said I was the only person she knew who could, literally, look down his nose at someone else. She had never meant that as a compliment, but at the moment it proved a useful skill.

The hostess did not, of course, find my name on her list. She left for a few moments, stopping about thirty feet away, where she discussed the matter with a penguin who was probably the supreme keeper of the gate. They had apparently concluded it was too risky to make a scene—or perhaps that there was some slight chance we might actually be legitimate; she returned and said, "Please follow me."

She led us across the room to a table of ten near the front. We were given two of the best seats in the house. But first she had to remove a pair of foreign diplomats from Tunisia who were suddenly at the wrong table. I noted their disgruntled frowns as another staff member relocated them to a spot near the rear of the room. Hairbun left us to the attentions of scurrying waiters, and the outright astonishment of eight strangers.

Colleen and I found ourselves in the company of an odd combination of British bankers and Greek shippers. I passed myself off as an American lawyer representing a start-up (and made up) multinational bank. Now conversing with bona fide bankers, I began to utter what had to have been a number of inane and disconnected words and phrases concerning banks, banking, lending, and interest. I suspect the two bankers at my table thought I was either a sociopath or a fraud, or perhaps both; the women, though, at least seemed intrigued.

Seeking friendlier company, I shifted my focus to the wives. The rest of the evening, in fact, I spent talking with the women. The husbands spoke with Colleen, who knew almost nothing of me and was therefore unable to satisfy their curious probes into my background.

While a regiment of waiters fussed over us, hurriedly bringing course after course (fish, delicate asparagus soup, lamb tidbits), so we might catch up with the others, four, flag-draped trumpeters on the dais entertained the guests with heraldic salutes. Then came toasts to the Queen, and even President Reagan. Someone introduced the U.S. Ambassador to the Court of St. James.

Dinner was everything one would expect . . . each exotic offering accompanied by a different wine, and at the end a flaming dessert. Besides a forest of wine glasses and endless pieces of silver and printed menus, at every setting lay a cassette recording of the evening's concert at Royal Albert Hall. Afterwards the gentlemen were given Cuban cigars.

I wondered if I'd ever again have such a sumptuous evening.

If others in the room had questions about us, they had a full hour to ask them during a series of backslapping, small-group photo sessions which followed the benediction. No questions were ever asked, but by then many guests were deep in their cups—and in any event there must have been a collective assumption that nobody who appeared as we did would risk attending such an affair unless he belonged to the odd branch of a family tree which knew nothing about protocol and decorum but somehow, perhaps by lineage alone, made these kinds of lists.

"We're off to catch the Concorde," I murmured to the photographer as I prepared to leave.

Colleen and I slipped away, and three blocks from the hotel, we burst into uncontainable laughter.

Several days later, at the official photographer's shop nearby, we picked up several 8x10 photos of us and our bedecked fellow revelers. I gave them all to Colleen, and she soon returned home to Dublin.

Years later, now married, I returned with my wife to the Savoy. It had much the same grandeur, but of course things were different. We came and went with no regard for the high tide, displaced no one when we took our room, and never thought to assume any identities but our own. We had pleasant, easy dealings with a great many people—without tension, or mystery, or any undercurrents of fraud.

In the end, it was strange to have entered and departed this near-perfect world just as I appeared to be—a professionally contented lawyer, whose brief and distant fling as a banker was surely displayed somewhere in the photo archives of the Savoy's glorious evenings past . . . along with the scowling photos of two diplomats from Tunisia.

Chapter Twenty-Nine

A Red Dress and Off to Town

IN MY OWN stubborn way, I wanted Bobby and Eric to live forever. Nobody else could keep them alive, but I could.

If the first and second versions of my memoir did not find a publisher, I'd try a third. I'd do whatever was needed—take classes, show it to all the smart people I knew, pay to have it formally critiqued.

The comments and critiques grew kinder, more laudatory; I sensed I was getting closer.

And then something unexpected happened. Thanks to my friend and agent, Pat Teal, who gave me the gentlest of nudges, I wired Saul Cohen, a prominent editor who'd turned down *Higher Than Eagles,* and I offered to write a different sort of book. He called back and said, "That's an interesting idea, a woman writing a hang gliding book. Why don't you send me a proposal?"

We said goodbye and I immediately called Pat. "What's a proposal?"

She tried to explain, but with scant clues on how you go about writing one, I sat at my typewriter and spewed out whatever came to mind: lists of everything I knew about hang gliding . . . a hasty first chapter . . . a few thoughts on topics. For days I did what I did shamelessly. I bluffed.

To my astonishment, Saul Cohen took me on!

It was like landing a whale in a rowboat.

HERE WAS ANOTHER peak, a moment when "ta da!" seemed the appropriate response . . . when you really should get out the red dress and go to town!

Soon I would be an author—*a book author! A Prentice-Hall author.* I looked back at my article-writing days as something distant and left behind, as though I'd crossed a very wide river. This was new land over here, elitist territory, and surely, surely, once arrived, an author would never again be forced to swim back across the river.

Over here, I imagined, books were easy to sell. Editors paid attention and rushed to offer contracts. Writing became synonymous with selling.

Oh, what a mystical world I'd created . . . but why not? Surely we're entitled to bask in our dreams, at least for a while.

The contract came, and then the check (half of ten thousand dollars), and the whole process was very New York and quite sophisticated and endlessly thrilling.

I told everyone I knew—every one of my hundreds of best friends.

And then reality hit. I was now required to write the book—a non-fiction based on history, research, and technical information . . . a radical departure from a manuscript drawn mostly from memories and experience.

A second reality followed the first. At least part of the manuscript would necessarily be devoted to man's early attempts at unpowered flight—about which I knew nothing.

Finally, having apparently convinced my editor that I was something of an expert on all things aeronautical, I had to write with flair and sound like an expert.

One night, about two A.M., it came to me that Prentice-Hall had presented me with a nasty choice: find a way to write the book or send back the contract.

Only an overly-conscientious, trouble-borrowing German given to interior monologues would find this an issue worth debating. After a few twitchy nights, I decided. Since bluffing had gotten me the job, bluffing would have to carry me the rest of the way.

I tipped the whale out of my rowboat and opted to become an expert.

AN EDITOR FRIEND, Gil Dodgen, helped. He, too, had jumped into a job he didn't know (as editor of a magazine), and his advice was steadying. "If you don't know what to do first, do *something.* The rest will come to you."

The library was the right place to start. With enough reading about the early days of unpowered flight (which was really the history of both airplanes and hang gliders), I *became* an expert. Research, besides being necessary, was strangely exhilarating.

I also made lists. Don't laugh. Lists are magic, they lift the confusion out of your brain and transfer it to paper. Lists create order out of chaos. Assigning different jobs to different weeks means you can worry in manageable increments—one week at a time.

Which led to another surprise. *Writing* a non-fiction is easy. All it requires is knowledge, logic, good grammar, and a massive determination to avoid producing even one boring paragraph.

It's the corollary jobs that get you . . . the sheer numbers involved: 150 photographs for which it's necessary to compose 150 captions—then add 150 page-references and photo credits. Plus several hundred permission letters, all with return envelopes.

Prentice-Hall was so fussy about permissions, if someone breathed on a paragraph, you had to get permission to use it.

Toward the end, the project kept snagging: sources for some of my best quotes could never be tracked down, so they had to be removed or paraphrased; the photos I'd struggled so hard to get multiplied like rabbits until I had far too many (though I'd paid for the excess); beautiful pictures became worthless when they couldn't be tied to text.

That summer Chris came home from medical school and, with

his usual efficiency, whipped out (or so it seemed to me), a section on "How to Fly."

THE FINAL WEEKS were lunacy. Except for the sweet edge of humor maintained by Betty-Jo, who assembled a 100-page Baedeker with the ease of a librarian cataloguing books, all attention was focused on the fever in my upstairs garret. Elsewhere in the house, civilized living vanished: laundry accumulated in hampers and overflowed and indoor plants drooped in despair and cried for water. I hardly noticed.

Dinners consisted of whatever Rob brought home from the nearest fast food take-out.

I remember the last days of typing. Nobody had computers back then. We all worked on typewriters, which meant no spell checks, no "delete" buttons, no "insert" capabilities and, worst of all, no "print" keys. One mistake in the wrong place meant you had to re-type the whole rotten page—or maybe several pages. Using a typewriter to crank out a manuscript was about the same, time-wise, as jumping on a horse to go to Palm Springs.

Though I'd stayed up all night, two days before it was due, the manuscript kept expanding like a soufflé, so that no matter how much or how fast I typed I still seemed to have about the same amount left to do.

My editor friend, Gil Dodgen, was arriving momentarily to pick up the manuscript so he could read it and write a jacket blurb, and I remember his getting there and finding me still frantically pounding out the last chapter.

I met him at the front door. Gil looked handsome, cool, pleasant.

After a night's binge with the typewriter, no lipstick, and my hair all stringy, I bore more than a passing resemblance to a witch. I dragged him to my upstairs study, where I worked in a narrow valley surrounded by several mountain ranges of stacked papers. He seemed mildly perplexed when he found no place to sit.

After a while he offered to help, and painfully conscious that I was wasting His Editorship's time, I put him to work collating. I should have sent him home, but I kept thinking any minute I would get the recalcitrant manuscript under control. Besides, he lived thirty minutes away and I didn't have time to make the drive.

An embarrassing amount of time later we finished, and Gil followed me to our local copy shop, where, I promised, "They'll run this right off and you can take your copy and go."

Southern California was in the midst of a heat wave, and what I didn't know right then was that photocopy machines get distemper when it's hot.

The shop owner, Fred, took my painfully-typed manuscript, stuck it in his machine, lowered the lid and pressed a button. For a while the machine hummed contentedly and spat out copies in orderly fashion. And then a red light flashed. Suddenly, with a snap of metal teeth, everything stopped. The motor stopped whirring and the machine gagged like a shark that bit the surfboard instead of the surfer.

Fred, a pleasant fellow, thin and dry, gingerly reached his arm into the bowels of the machine and extracted a jammed paper. It was crumpled and distorted. I assumed it was one of the copies.

I assumed wrong. A closer look revealed it was an original. I glanced at Gil, horrified. He'd seen it too. But neither of us said anything. Fred tried to smooth out the wrinkles.

Then he started his machine again, and now it was only a short time before it gagged once more and Fred withdrew another ruined sheet. When the third and fourth crunched-up sheets came out of the machine, Gil whispered, "The first time it happened after fifty pages. We're getting down to about one in four."

By now I was in a state of shocked denial. The machine was crunching my manuscript at a rate of one-in-four and I was standing there numb, watching the destruction as though the pages belonged to someone else.

Even Fred looked distressed. I finally roused enough to speak up. "My manuscript is all wrinkled . . . I can't use it like that."

The man extracted the rest of the pages. "I'll hand-feed them on the other copier," he said, at which Gil remarked that he really ought to be going.

The situation had worsened dramatically. Now I would not only have to re-type great portions of the book, but also drive it to Gil's house. However, I was too tired to work up a decent angst.

It was Fred who responded, "It won't take me long now," at which Gil shuffled his feet and shrugged. "Well . . . I've waited this long . . ."

"I'm sorry," I said. "I should have let you go."

The hand-feeding ended shortly and Gil left with the only decent copy of my book.

I said to Fred, "What am I going to do with all these wrinkled pages?" I knew too well, but I wanted him to face up to it.

He scratched his head and studied the crumpled sheets. I waited and he waited. Finally he said, as though the problem were solved, "You can iron them."

For a moment I didn't think I'd heard him right. *Iron my manuscript?* I'd been up all night typing it and now I was supposed to go home and *iron* it? I stared at Fred in disbelief. I didn't iron my clothes!

He went on. "Use a steam iron. It smoothes out the cotton content in the paper." He felt one of the wrinkled sheets with a knowing finger.

I had no intention of quibbling that the last time I used my steam iron it coughed once and then spat rusty water all over the fabric, turning it a darkish red. I just stood there, speechless.

Things were about as bad as they could get. I wasn't sure what to do next.

That's when Fred made his first reasonable suggestion. Maybe he didn't want me committing suicide in his shop.

"Tell you what. I'll reprint your wrinkled pages on heavy bond paper. They'll look just like the originals. Just as good." He wore a happier look.

Relief washed over me sweetly, and all at once the day looked so much better I didn't ask, *Why are you just now thinking of this?*

With new purpose, Fred re-ran the wrinkled sheets. And they did look like the originals. One would hardly know.

THE MANUSCRIPT WENT off to Prentice-Hall the next day and I was free of it for several months. But soon the project had its tentacles around me again. On December 15 the galley proofs arrived for final review. Prentice-Hall decreed it was time to make an index . . . and everything was due back within a week.

All of which suggests if you intend to become an author, you can forget about minor events like Christmas.

Though hang gliding pilots flocked to get the published book, and reviewers were more than kind, the rest of the world hardly knew it existed, so *Manbirds: Hang Gliders and Hang Gliding,* never made any best-seller lists. However, I will always love *Library Journal* for putting it on their list of the year's 100-best books in Science and Technology.

Though I'm probably the only person that noticed.

FOR ME, BOBBY and Eric do indeed live on. All I need do is begin reading *Higher Than Eagles* (which sold years later), to find them again in my memories, laughing and flying lyrically and committing all the outrageous pranks that I now find funny.

At last, after nine published books (and four written but never sold), I've acceded to Rob's demand that I use my education to bring in money—perhaps $150,000 by now—which, after years of effort, figures out to so little per hour I try not to think about it.

Rob says occasionally, "Almost any other job would have earned you more." But he says it with a certain pride.

Anyway, as I tell him from time to time, "If I hadn't been writing all those years, I would have been at Nordstrom's *spending* $150,000."

Maralys made the talk shows with her new book, *Manbirds.*

CHAPTER THIRTY

Renovating the House

NOBODY COULD UNDERSTAND why we were adding on to the house. "Your children are pretty much grown," a friend pointed out reasonably enough. "Why do you need more space?"

Rob answered with a grin, "We always add a room whenever a kid leaves. Makes perfect sense to us. When all the kids are gone, we'll build a castle."

I nodded. "Well actually," I said, "I got tired of eating breakfast on top of yesterday's mail. I know it's ridiculous—spending eighty-thousand dollars for a place to put the mail. But we don't pretend to be rational."

The question of whose idea it was to expand the whole rear of the house and add a breakfast room shifted from week to week. In Rob's mind "our idea" became "her idea" as the kitchen began to resemble a hobo's digs, with appliances missing everywhere, like a mouth with half its teeth, and exposed water pipes staring at us from the sub flooring, and the walls sporting nail holes but no cabinets. It continued to be "her idea" as I hauled buckets of dirty dishes to the bathtub and the temperature in the open part of the house dropped below forty and a raccoon came in, and I do mean in. There he was one night in the family room, standing his ground defiantly, eyeing us through his mask.

It became "our project" once more as the kitchen and family room began to look sleek and modern, twice as nice as before—and "her idea" again as the stonemasons arrived to build new lower and upper patios. The latest crew muddied and tore up the backyard as they worked, so that cement-laden dirt began creeping into the house through several doorways.

"It looks like an abandoned brickyard out there," Rob declared as we faced Thanksgiving with multi-colored bricks piled haphazardly around the yard and mud lurking outside all the doors, just daring us to step outside.

"This has been an unbearable year," he declared, and vowed he would absolutely never do anything major to the house again, come hell or high water . . . and high water was what we seemed in danger of getting, because the toilets in two mostly unused bathrooms had developed small leaks, and water began seeping onto the floors when we weren't looking, and the bathroom floors were slowly rotting into mush. I expected to go back there one day and step right through the sub floor onto the dirt.

And sure enough, it wasn't long before we had to tear up the bathrooms, too.

The house renovations began to consume all aspects of my life. One morning, for instance, I had to go to Ralph's Market to load up on empty cardboard boxes so I could pack up and move everything out of the bathroom cupboards—of which we had two dozen. While I was adding rolls of paper towels, I managed to topple about seven huge boxes out of my grocery cart right into the path of an aristocratic-looking lady who, nonplussed, smiled and said, "Looks like you've hit the mother lode of boxes."

I laughed. "You must be a writer," I said, hoping she was and we might get acquainted. But she merely smiled again and moved on.

Then for some reason I kept crossing paths with the same lady throughout the store, privately amused that she gave me and my overloaded cart wider and wider berth.

But she was nowhere around when I became truly reckless and gave my cart an excessive push—and sent it crashing into someone's untended grocery basket. Down in my duck blind of boxes I honestly hadn't seen the other wagon—and now I quickly backed off before the noise collected a crowd.

Well, I didn't collect a crowd, I collected "her."

Out from behind the bread she came, eyeing me in disbelief.

As she retrieved her cart from its bashing, she gave me a last, funny little look and said, more to herself than me, "I knew I should have come in the afternoon."

She sent me out of the store laughing, but also full of regret I would never get to know this witty lady better. Whereas I could envision us becoming friends, she would make certain the two of us were never in the same store again.

AS PART OF our house renovation, Rob and I eventually acquired a cavalier spirit, a "what the hell" attitude which spread like recklessly sown seeds over the entire house and meant we bought things we didn't necessarily need, like new living room drapes.

The old drapes might never have become part of the family history had Rob's car not failed just then, forcing him to borrow Kirk's disreputable Cutlass. Finding the driver's seat literally agape at the seams, Rob searched for something to throw over it—the closest thing at hand being one of the discarded draperies. Rob tossed the drape over the seat, letting the hooks dangle free in back. Since the car was, as usual, out of fuel, he headed for the nearest gas station.

As Rob drove he felt the drape slipping, working its way down the seat. When he got out of the car to pump gas he knew at once he wasn't alone; the drape had come with him.

It took only seconds to grasp the situation: the hooks had managed to embed themselves in the back of his bulky-knit Scottish sweater, and now here he was, standing in the gas station with a ten-foot-long, open-weave, gold-threaded cape flowing from his shoulders . . . and not only that, it was pleated!

Rob realized immediately he had a serious personal appearance problem. He glanced around, all too aware that he bore a remarkable similarity to King Henry the Eighth. Reaching around to disentangle himself, he quickly found that the hooks had dug in with fiendish cunning, just at that point in his back where he couldn't reach. He twirled and squirmed and shimmied, but all his efforts to free himself merely drew attention to his bizarre predicament.

As he spun around in his dangling cape, other customers began reacting with startled double-takes, then fast aversions of the eyes. The man fueling the nearest car stood at an odd angle, trying to keep one eye on the gas nozzle and the other on Rob. Rob knew all too well what the man was thinking. *I've gotta get away from this nut case.*

There are times when Rob's sense of humor utterly fails him, and this was one of them. Ever more exasperated, he clawed at his shoulders like a demented Shakespearian monarch. But the more frantic he became, the more the hooks behaved like porcupine quills, tightening their grip, until it appeared Rob might be wearing the living-room drapes for the rest of the day.

By now a few customers were quietly leaving the gas station, some without filling their tanks, and Rob was truly desperate. He considered disrobing right there among the gas pumps, pulling sweater and drape up over his head and ridding himself of both. But the sweater was tight and hard to remove under normal conditions, and the drape was so long it dragged the sweater down in back, and he couldn't begin to shed the two without scissors or a chain saw. Besides, he didn't like the idea of adding a strip tease to the rest of his already-underappreciated performance.

Feeling anything but regal, he kept his head down and filled his tank. Finished, he gathered his remaining dignity, strode purposefully across the station, paid the bill to a clerk who refused to look him in the eye, and sauntered back, trailing his cape as if it were his normal attire.

Once at home he walked into the house muttering, "Here, Babe, get me out of this damn thing!"

I took one look at his drifting, open-weave raiment and burst out laughing. I was laughing so hard it was difficult to make my fingers do what they had to do. "How did you happen to acquire this lovely garment?" I asked.

"Well, it certainly wasn't deliberate!"

The next time I saw the draperies they were heaped in a trash barrel near the curb, which, considering who put them there, was an act of wanton recklessness. For the man who never throws out anything, trashing those drapes indicated profound disgust, and meant he never, ever, wanted to see them again.

THE RENOVATION WAS finally finished.

I took a deep breath as Rob led us all out to the gracious wide steps that led to our new upper patio. He posed us along the steps in tiers, lining us up for another family photograph. In the early years of our marriage I'd asked Rob occasionally, "Why are we always interrupting what we're doing to take pictures?"

He never answered that question—he just gave me a look and said, "Turn this way, Babe. Now smile."

By 1981 I saw what Rob had done for us. All those years he'd been snapping pictures and adding captions—labeling the kids, labeling us, labeling our activities. He'd been keeping track . . . making a record of our lives.

As we posed that December of 1981, I was acutely aware once again that neither Eric nor Bobby were there, and for a moment I felt the lump that was always so quick to rise in my throat.

Yet there were others on the steps I was just getting to know . . . Bobby's sturdy little boy, now almost four, and Chris's two elfin girls. Later that morning Rob and I would take the two little girls out to breakfast, and I would listen to their whispery conversations and think, *Oh, Lord, these are darling kids.*

I realized our family would go on.

And I would more than survive.

THE END

It's hard to get the mob together, even on the new hardscape.

Epilogue

Rob's judgment about the "kids" who took over Wills Wings was right, and none of my fears came true. Under their enthusiastic management, Wills Wings not only maintained the quality that had mattered so much to Bobby and Chris, it also became the world's largest manufacturer of hang gliders. Who would have imagined such a thing? . . . that somehow the *kids* would accomplish what our family had never been able to do—grow the company and even turn a profit.

As an adult, Tracy spilled over with the same ebullience and natural persuasiveness that led the family into so many adventures. She earned an MBA, helped set up a surgi-center, and ultimately became the mayor of Tustin. She was elected to the top job four different years, and later to important regional boards. Widowed in the early 90's (her husband, Geoff, died of melanoma), she raised her two children alone—for more years than any of us wanted. Ten years later, she met and married Brad Hagen.

After Chris married Betty-Jo and they had the first of four children, he became a surgeon. As he said about his medical school class, "All the jocks ended up in orthopedics." Unable to resist his love of flying forever, Chris eventually built and now flies his own conventional airplane. For a long time he jokingly referred to Tracy as "my-sister-the-mayor." But that didn't stop him from cajoling her out of one of her mayor's badges, which he keeps in his car to impress any official who might be looking in the window.

Kenny became a trial attorney and lives in Norfolk, Virginia, with his wife and three daughters. His London capers ensured that adventures and travel would become important features of his life. Kenny no longer finds it necessary to look down his nose at anyone. In court he accomplishes with rhetoric what he once achieved with a haughty stare.

Our youngest, Kirk, has not done well. His foray into alcohol and drugs led him down a path from which he has not yet recovered, a sad journey I covered in my book, *Save My Son.* Yet we never give up hope. Some day, surely, I will write a follow-up story that celebrates his conquest of addiction.

Thanks to the big-voiced family members—Rob, Chris, Kenny, and Tracy, four raconteurs—our group reunions rollick with a wild flavor of unbridled energy that turns me into a wallflower. Since I cannot compete with all that outpouring of energy and humor, I am content to sit, laugh, and listen. But hey, I get even with them in time. If they're not careful, the craziest of what they do and say will end up in a story.

About the Author

Maralys Wills has lived three distinct lives: author of nine published books, teacher of college students, and mother of six children—five boys and a girl.

Wills attended Stanford and UCLA, earning both a B.A. in psychology and her teaching credentials. She also helped run her sons' hang glider manufacturing business, but after multiple family tragedies, she decided to return home and write books. Her most challenging writing project, a memoir titled *Higher Than Eagles,* became her biggest triumph, garnering excellent reviews and five movie options.

For the last nineteen years, Wills has taught novel-writing on the college level, and in 2000 she was voted Teacher of the Year. In addition to frequent speaking engagements, she has given numerous writing seminars across the country. She currently lives and writes in Santa Ana, California.

Visit the author's website at *www.maralys.com.*